ADRENALINE

and

STRESS

ADRENALINE
and
STRESS

Dr. Archibald D. Hart

THOMAS NELSON
Since 1798

For other products and live events,
visit us at: thomasnelson.com

ADRENALINE AND STRESS
by Dr. Archibald Hart.

Library of Congress Cataloging-in-Publication Data

Hart, Archibald D.
    Adrenaline and stress / Archibald D. Hart.
      p. cm.
    ISBN 0-8499-3690-X
    1. Adrenaline—Physiological effect. 2. Stress (Psychology)—Prevention.
3. Christian life. I. Title II. Title: Adrenaline and stress.
QP572.A27H37 1985 613
                                      85-22507
                                          CIP

Printed in the United States of America
07 08 QW 18 17 16 15

Acknowledgments

To my grandfather, Archibald Daniel Hart, who first taught me how to live a balanced life . . .

To my wife, Kathleen, who continues to teach me how to be a whole person . . .

To my secretary, Nova Hutchins, who faithfully and with the spirit of Christ has helped me revise and update this manuscript . . .

To my colleagues at Fuller Theological Seminary, who provide personal and professional encouragement . . .

. . . I say *thank you.*

—Dr. Archibald D. Hart

List of Figures

Contents

Part Three: Healing Your "Hurry Sickness"

Preface

This book is for hurried people—for normal people who live busy but sometimes hectic lives.

It is for those who strive for excellence in all they do and find there is just not enough time in the day to accomplish what they desire.

It is for all those who drive themselves hard and strive to be the best they can be. (This includes mothers as well as bank managers, followers as well as leaders.)

It is for those who must be creative and take the initiative to achieve their goals.

In short, this book is for those who try to live life to the fullest—in business, ministry, the professions, trades, or school. It is also for me, because I also need to heed its message!

Most of us live with a sense of time urgency, as well as a sense that we must do something meaningful with our lives. Because life is so short and opportunities are limited, many of us hurry through life at a frantic pace, with little tolerance for anything that blocks our goals or delays our accomplishments. We devote little time to the pursuit of spiritual things, and we chase ourselves to an early grave by ignoring the effect that "hurry sickness" can have on our minds and bodies.

We misunderstand the nature of stress, despite the fact that we have been deluged in recent years with books and magazine articles on the subject. We have been inundated with information about what to eat, whom to avoid, how to exercise, and when to take vacations. Most of this information, we ignore.

But what we have not heard clearly enough is that the essence of stress damage lies not so much in the problems of life, but in our attitude toward time and the excitement and pleasure we derive from interesting challenges and demanding schedules. The stress response is a natural form of arousal. In moderation, it is healthy—even necessary. But continuous overarousal leads to stress disease—and it doesn't matter whether this is the consequence of overwork, unhappiness, or plain, old-fashioned excitement. Such long-term overarousal and the excessive flow of those hormones associated with stress will eventually lead to physiological and psychological distress, and the leader among these hormones is adrenaline.

Recent research has made it very clear that hyperarousal of the adrenal system is the essential causative factor in coronary and artery disease, the most serious form of stress damage. (Of course, cholesterol also plays an important role. But in the absence of excessive adrenaline, cholesterol and other well-known factors seldom cause heart disease.)

In addition to coronary and artery disease, many other kinds and symptoms of stress damage can be traced back to the excessive flow of adrenaline: headaches (tension and migraine), gastric problems, ulcers, and high blood pressure. I believe, therefore, that there is a need for one more book on the topic of stress, a book designed to help us control the stress problem at its very fountainhead—our adrenal systems.

Can we learn to control adrenaline production? Can we so manage our thinking, attitudes, and behavior that we can reduce the excessive arousal of this hormone and thus avoid the damaging consequences of living life in high gear? Can we so live at peace with ourselves that we get out of the fast lane and actually overcome the tendency to respond to life as if it were one long "emergency?"

My answer is a definite and resounding "Yes." The techniques I will describe in this book can be summarized by the term, "adrenaline management." The underlying idea is that just as we can learn to control our habits and behaviors, we can also learn to control our tendency to recruit excessive adrenaline and keep it within less destructive limits.

Ever since the late 1930s, when Dr. Hans Selye, the great originator of stress research, first highlighted the connection between stress and the adrenal hormones in the bodies of animals, there has been a growing conviction among many that the overproduction of adrenaline and related hormones is the primary cause of stress disease. My own work supports this conviction. For the past twenty years I have worked extensively with stressed patients, developing therapeutic techniques (including those known as "biofeedback") to help people reduce stress symptoms. I have also undertaken a number of research projects in collaboration with my doctoral-level students, looking at the causes and cures for overstress. As a result, I have come to see the adrenaline response as providing a powerful key to unlocking the mystery of stress.

I believe the approach I will take here is unique. It is now becoming accepted that the excessive flow of adrenaline is the essential factor in stress disease, even to the extent that some have suggested the use of medication to control its overproduction as an aid to stress management. To my knowledge, however, no one has yet proposed a method such as this, whereby adrenaline production can be controlled by psychological methods.

On the stress management scene, a set of techniques called "Type-A Personality Counseling" has emerged. This technique is similar in intent to what I will propose here, except that it is directed specifically to a limited set of behaviors performed by those individuals who have a "Type-A Personality." "Adrenaline management," as I perceive it, is important for all of us, regardless of our basic personality type.

While I don't want to fall into the trap of making unreasonable promises, I believe that if my counsel is faithfully followed it will significantly reduce your tendency to develop stress disease. And you can possibly also reverse to a significant extent the stress damage you have already suffered. I know, because not only have I applied these techniques to myself with effective results, but I have also used them extensively in my practice as a clinical psychologist specializing in stress management.

For some of you, adrenaline management will mean unlearning an "addiction" to your own adrenaline; you may have become so dependent on the "high" your adrenaline supplies that you may have difficulty giving it up. For others, adrenaline management will mean discovering more effective and efficient ways of accomplishing creative tasks—methods other than continually "psyching" yourself up to a high level of arousal. For a few, it will mean learning how to increase your adrenaline flow when it is needed in a particular life crisis, because you may tend to be too "hang loose."

For all of us, adrenaline management will mean learning how to control our bodies by "holding back" when we want to conserve our energy and "letting go" when an extra "push" is needed.

By learning to balance our adrenaline production, we can achieve maximum energy and freedom to live a full and stress-free life.

—Archibald D. Hart, Ph.D.
Pasadena, California

Introduction
to the Revised Edition

It is now almost ten years since I wrote this, my most popular, book. During these years I have received scores of letters and have listened as many people told me the same story, namely, "Your book saved my life!"

I usually respond by saying, "It saved *my* life as well, because I have practiced its principles for many years now and as a consequence am less stressed and more peaceful than I would have been had I not. I am probably the greatest beneficiary of its contents."

I once lived in the fastest of all lanes. I took pride in being able to do things faster than anyone—including walking and talking. I hated wasting time and was agitated by people who talked slowly. Waiting in line made me nervous. I hurried about, wore precision wrist watches, and preferred cars that could out-gun others from take-off at traffic lights. But, most destructively, I relished competition almost to the point of being combative. Anyone who challenged me was my enemy and had to be conquered.

But more than ten years ago I made peace with myself and resolved to take control of the stress that was killing me. How did I do it? It's all described in this book. And what I have found is that I am not less effective, but more efficient; not less energized, but able to conserve my energy by understanding when it is being wasted and when it needs to be reserved.

The time has come for me to revise and update this book. The essential principles remain the same. Ten years of experience have confirmed every point I originally made, both through my successes and my failures—and there have been several. A few patients who came to me, asking for help who had either already had a heart attack or knew they were stressed to the point of breaking, died of heart attacks or strokes while we were trying to get their stress under control. In every instance, without exception, their demise resulted from a violation of the principles outlined in this book.

Over the years I have carefully scrutinized the ideas originally presented and have tried to learn from patients I have treated. My revisions reflect the consequent conclusions. If my tone seems more urgent or forceful, it is only because I feel more convinced than ever that we can beat the stress problem before it destroys us. I have often enough seen dramatic changes take place in the most stressed men and women. I am thoroughly convinced that commitment to change one's lifestyle and a little bit of know-how can have lifesaving results. This book provides the know-how. *You* must provide the commitment!

PART ONE

Adrenaline Arousal—
The Essence Of Stress Disease

"No one can live without experiencing some degree of stress. You may think that only serious disease or intensive physical or mental injury can cause stress. This is false. Crossing a busy intersection, exposure to a draft, or even sheer joy are enough to activate the body's stress mechanism to some extent. Stress is not even necessarily bad for you; it is also the spice of life, for any emotion, any activity, causes stress."

—HANS SELYE
The Stress of Life

Understanding the Nature of Stress

We are entering an extraordinary new age in medicine and the health sciences. On the one hand, we are making remarkable progress in curing illnesses and prolonging life. On the other hand, we are losing the battle against a very simple but elusive problem—stress. Despite medical science's enormous strides in treating illness, the problems caused by stress are becoming more prevalent and difficult to treat. The time is rapidly approaching, if it hasn't already arrived, when we will be dying less and less from infectious or invasive diseases—but more often from the ravaging effects of too much stress. And stress disease is different from most forms of illness—we bring it on ourselves!

It's not that we don't know stress is a problem! Our predicament is that we don't really understand the nature of stress or how it does its damage. Therefore, we don't know how to prevent that damage. And stress disease, for the most part, can be avoided.

At the very core of the stress problem is our Western, twentieth-century lifestyle. Of course, parts of the East are just as stress-ridden, but I am focusing on our unique approach to life and the stress it causes.

The lives of most of us are far too hectic and fast-paced. We are driven by a need to succeed, and a very distinctive need to prove ourselves. This leaves little room for relaxation or leisure in our hectic lives. It's as if we are trapped on a runaway train and don't know where the brakes are. The engines of our bodies have jammed at full throttle.

Juliet Schor, a professor of economics at Harvard University, recently published a fascinating book entitled *The Overworked American.*[1] In it she accurately portrays the underlying reason for why our culture is so overstressed: there has been an un-anticipated decline in leisure in both work and home life. She debunks the conventional wisdom that before modern times, the majority of people worked from sunup to sundown, 365 days a year, a myth that is often used to encourage people to work even harder. Leisure time in the ancient world was plentiful and those who tilled the soil (the majority) had long periods of inactivity over the winter. It is only in modern times, following the industrial revolution, that longer, more arduous—and, of course, more stressful—work patterns developed. And even in very recent times we have seen yet a further decline of leisure, of the kind that is needed to counteract stress disease. Both men and women, especially women, work longer hours now than they did two decades ago. The evidence for this is well documented in Dr. Schor's book, so I don't have to belabor the point here.

The bottom line is that our priorities are all unbalanced. Our super time consciousness, the pace of life in general, and the prevalence of "hurry sickness" are all detrimental to our well-being. Most of us need to relax more, learn how to unwind, and stop and smell the roses occasionally—all important protections against the damage stress can cause. In this book I hope to be able to show some ways the reader can achieve a balance between productivity and play, pressure and pleasure, and especially a balance between a life of unavoidable propulsion and peacefulness.

WHAT IS STRESS, ANYWAY?

The word *stress* means different things to different people. It is a multifaceted response that includes changes in perception, emotions, behavior, and physical functioning. Some think of it only as tension: others view it as anxiety. Some think of it as good, others as bad. The truth is that we all need a certain amount of stress to keep us alive, although too much becomes harmful to us. (When most of us use the term *stress,* we are usually referring to this harmful aspect—overstress. In this book, I will try to distinguish between the many confusing terms used for stress.)

Let's look at some examples that will help us better understand the true nature of stress:

- You only have ten minutes to get to work because you've overslept, and it usually takes you at least twenty! The boss is counting on you to chair an important meeting first thing, so you really need to be there on time. And to make matters worse, you can't find your wallet and car keys. You search frantically, losing precious seconds as you become more upset about being late. You become impatient, then angry. You are under STRESS.

- You have been thinking of going back to school to finish your degree, but it has been a long time since you've been in a classroom setting. You're not sure whether you can handle schoolwork on top of your other responsibilities. At the same time, you feel the need for some kind of change in your life. So you stew over your dilemma, unable to make a decision. You are under STRESS.

- As you drive to an appointment, the freeway is more crowded than usual. You decide to change lanes because the other seems to be going faster. But Murphy's Law kicks in. Traffic slows down the moment you enter the lane! So you find the traffic is even slower in the new lane than the one you abandoned. You become irritated and mumble a few choice, but very private, words under your breath. You are under STRESS.

- You've just seen your husband off to work with the kids he has to deliver to school. You settle down to enjoy a cup of coffee in peace . . . when the telephone rings. It's your mother. She's not feeling well and wants to know if you will take her to the doctor. You had planned on doing something else, and your mother's intrusion into your plans really irritates you. But what can you do? You smile politely (even though she can't see you), say a few kind words you don't really mean, and go get dressed. You are under STRESS.

- The boss comes to your desk with a smile on her face. "You've been doing a really great job," she says, and you know immediately she's setting you up for something. "I would like you to do a special project for me." *Here it comes!* "If you do a good job on this one, there will be others like it in the future. Want to give it a try?" "Sure!" you reply, trying to sound enthusiastic. This could be the break you've been waiting for! You begin to feel a surge of excitement. Time for an extra cup of coffee to get the juices flowing even stronger. You plan on working late, so you call the family to tell them not to expect you for dinner. You are under STRESS.

These are all examples of stress. The first four are easily recognized as such, but many would not view the last example as stressful. We mistakenly think that if an activity is exciting or challenging, it is not stressful. Nothing could be further from the truth. Even though you may love your work and rise to a new challenge, adrenaline excitement can still lead to stress—especially if it never gets a break. So if the stress caused by excitement is allowed to continue uninterrupted for too long, the process that leads to stress disease will set in.

THE BODY'S ALARM SYSTEM

We live within a body that responds to stress . . . in a world that produces it. The potential for stress is all about us—in our friends, family, work, in every part of life. Our bodies are intricately designed to respond to stress in such a way as to help us cope with it, at least initially. Each of us is equipped with a highly sophisticated defense system designed to help protect against threats that would destroy us and to help us cope with those events that would challenge us. This stress response system is comprised of a complex array of hormones and instinctive responses that ensures our survival.

Now what is crucial to understand is that this fantastic stress response system can be triggered by anything that creates a state of arousal or alarm in our bodies—anything that mobilizes our bodies' defenses against hostile, threatening, or even challenging events in our environment. These threatening or challenging events actually don't have to take place or be real. Often it is enough simply to imagine them. Isn't that amazing? The stress response cannot tell the difference between real and imagined threats; it responds the same way to both sets of stimuli.

Now, the greater the mobilization of this stress defense system, the greater the potential for overstress and, therefore, for stress damage. There is a direct connection.

When the state of alarm or emergency is triggered, our various physiological systems are bathed in adrenaline which disrupts normal functioning and produces a heightened state of arousal. In the immediate "emergency" situation the heart beats faster, digestion is speeded up, and many hormones are released into the bloodstream. All of this takes place for one—and only one—reason: to prepare us to deal with the emergency. Every other function is put on hold!

I will describe these changes in a little more detail later on. For now, we just need to understand that very sophisticated system of defense that has been designed into us. It is extremely complex and we merely have to cooperate with it, so this system meant for our good will not turn against us and destroy us in the process of protecting us. One system that functions in this manner is the body's "auto-immune" system. When it is allowed to *do its thing,* it protects us. When we abuse it, it turns against us. Many stress-related disorders are the consequences of the body turning against itself.

Whenever we are threatened physically or psychologically, a chain of responses is set in motion to prepare us for what has been described as the "fight or flight" response. More accurately, it should be called the "fight, fright, or flight response." It's as simple as that. When we are under stress, any stress, we are prepared to attack what is threatening us, run away from it, or just go into an extreme state of fear or panic. Behind it all is our wonderful adrenal system with its complex assortment of hormones, all designed to do something or other.

The system triggered by stress is called the "alarm system." Its purpose is to alert us to any threat or challenge so that we can be better equipped to deal with it.

But difficulties arise when we are threatened over and over again, or when we are constantly challenged, or when we live in a perpetual state of emergency. When this happens, what was designed as a protective agent begins to be harmful to us. This is when ordinary stress begins to damage us.

The clearest way I can illustrate this is to ask you to imagine an elastic band. If it is stretched between your thumbs and then quickly released, it easily returns to its normal, relaxed position. The body's stress response is also "stretched" whenever it is subjected to an emergency or demand. It ought to return to a normal, relaxed state when the emergency is over. But if the elastic band is stretched and then held in an extended position for a long period of time, it begins to lose its elastic properties and does not return to its former relaxed state. It develops hairline cracks and will eventually snap.

Similarly, if our bodies are repeatedly held in a constant state of alarm, they soon begin to show this loss of elasticity, with damaging consequences. So-called psychosomatic disorders, which have both physical and psychological causes, are often consequences of this loss of resilience.

HOW DOES STRESS CAUSE ILLNESS?

While this question will be explored more fully in the next chapter, some comments are appropriate here. Research conducted over many years has clearly shown that one way excessive stress can cause illness is by undermining the body's immunological defense mechanisms. In other words, too much stress reduces the body's immune system and thus weakens its ability to fight off disease. The result is that viruses and bacteria thrive in a highly stressed body. This does not take place immediately. The process takes place slowly, eventually robbing the immune system of just enough "fighting power" to place us in jeopardy for illnesses, both minor and major. There is even some suspicion that stress may cause some forms of cancer to grow more rapidly because the body's ability to fight off the growth of cancerous cells is dependent on its own immune system. Some cancer treatments actually use the reverse of this process to aid the body in fighting cancer. In other words, whatever can be used to increase the immune system, including the growth of special cells and stress management, is effective in assisting the treatment of cancer!

In addition to hindering the body's defense systems, stress can also lead to illness by disrupting normal functions more directly and damaging the tissue of the body. For example, the increased secretion of acid in the stomach irritates and eats away the stomach lining. This eventually leads to inflammation or ulcers.

There is an even more subtle way in which stress can cause illness. The high level of adrenaline sparked by stress reduces our ability to rest. It cuts down on our apparent need for sleep, and creates poor eating habits. All this can lead to increased usage of drugs, alcohol, cigarettes, and other damaging substances. These, in turn, can take their toll by causing further illnesses and damage in and of themselves. So too much stress can set in motion a long chain of destructive side effects. Is it any wonder more people are dying of its total influence today than from almost any other cause?

NOT ALL STRESS IS BAD!

I am always reluctant to talk about the positive aspects of stress because some quickly jump to using it as an excuse to rationalize their own high-stress lives.

But yes, some stress is good for us. Not much . . . but some! I must emphasize, however, that chances are *good* that your stress is mostly *bad*. There is just too much influence of our fast-track world on most of us for it to not be so.

Stress is not damaging to everybody all the time. Sometimes we thrive on stress. We experience it as exhilaration. It fires our boilers and motivates us to get projects completed or to overcome obstacles that block our achievements.

Every athlete knows how important it is to get into the right psychological frame of mind before a game or event. At certain times and at certain levels, stress can enhance a person's concentration, strength, and productivity. The heightened energy we get from a surge of adrenaline can even save our lives in an emergency—just as it is meant to do.

But stress is only *good* if it is short lived. An exciting baseball game, for instance, is time-limited so the thrill of excitement comes and goes quickly. A challenge is met, then passes away.

The "ebb and flow" of our adrenaline is crucial to effective living, and we must keep it in mind as we design a healthy lifestyle for ourselves. This means that periods of high demand must be followed by periods of low arousal so as to allow the adrenal system time for rejuvenation. If this doesn't happen, even good stress can turn bad. We must learn to enjoy the valleys of low arousal (even boredom) in order to more thoroughly enjoy the mountain peaks of excitement without incurring damage.

Good stress (also called *eustress,* from the Latin *eu,* meaning "good") is positive and helpful only because it is not experienced continuously. It excites, but then relaxes the system back to normal quickly. If there is never a time when the demand for stress is passed so that the body can return to a state of low arousal, rest, and recovery, the result will be *bad* stress or *distress,* from the Latin *dis,* meaning "bad"), no matter how good the heightened state of stress may feel.

On the matter of how good stress can enhance athletic performance, one other recent development has helped us come to understand the limits of "good" stress. Highly motivated athletes soon discover that too much adrenaline actually works against them. The wrong muscles become tense and work against the muscles that are needed. Adrenaline can become exhausted at a critical or final moment. So, in recent years the field of "sports psychology" has come into being. Sports psychologists essentially help athletes to maximize their performance by teaching them how to relax and not waste adrenaline on unnecessary activities. Stress management is an essential part of every sport psychologist's armament. The principles of enhancing sporting prowess can also be applied to everyday living, as we will see as we proceed.

The effect of those threats created by worry and anxiety are also worth noting here. There are people whose thoughts are so active and bothersome that they constantly imagine the worst. This worry magnifies actual threats and creates imagined ones—both of which trigger the stress response. And because they are imagined or blown out of proportion, these threats cannot be confronted or easily resolved.

The problem is in the mind, although for the body the imagined threat is interpreted as real. Furthermore, we don't always recognize our worries as stressors. They hide in the dark recesses of our minds and come out to haunt us during the early hours of the morning when we are trying to get to sleep again after being awakened by some noise. Or it plays like a broken record in the background of our unconscious while we do our daily chores.

It is these more subtle threats that produce the greatest amount of stress damage. Things that worry, scare, or frighten us, even though they only exist in our thoughts, are stress-producing because there is little we can do to fight vague, imagined threats. This is why they can be the most destructive of all. We don't know where or who the enemy is! "Let not your heart be troubled, neither let it be afraid" (John 14:27) is not only a worthy religious sentiment, it is a powerful antidote to stress disease!

"HIDDEN STRESS"

Another factor that complicates the stress picture is that of "hidden stress" or, more accurately, "hidden stressors."

We cannot always feel distress when we are, in fact, experiencing it. This is because we are all born with an amazing human trait—that of adaptability. Our bodies have the remarkable ability to adjust to a wide variety of conditions, from heat to cold, high and low altitudes, hard physical work or sedentary inactivity. For instance, if I walk into a dark room from the bright sunlight, at first I cannot see anything. But as my eyes get used to the darkness, I begin to see quite clearly. Similarly, if I now leave the dark room and go back into the sunlight, I will at first be blinded but soon my eyes will adjust and once again I will be able to see. This adaptability operates in every system of the body. We can get used to almost every variety of living conditions because of it, but not without some penalty.

There is a negative side to all this wonderful adaptability. Our bodies can adapt to circumstances that in the long run are harmful to us—such as when we carry too much stress for too long a period of time. After a while we get so used to it, we no longer recognize it for what it really is—*distress*. Forgotten and unrecognized, it does its work of destruction nevertheless!

For example, let's take the stress that raises blood pressure. Anger does it very easily. If the anger is not resolved quickly, the body will adapt to the higher level of arousal just as easily as your body would adjust to the heat and arid climate if you moved to live in the Sahara Desert. The blood pressure goes up and stays up—and will not come down very easily again. It is all a part of our adaptation capabilities, only here the adaptation is destructive. Our blood vessels cannot tolerate elevated blood pressure for long periods of time. This type of blood pressure problem is called "essential hypertension," and I know it well. Twenty years ago I suffered from it!

Simply stated, when you experience a lot of stress for a long time, your body adapts to this prolonged stress by keeping you in a protracted state of "fight or flight." This is one reason why some people have high blood pressure, although at any given moment their overall life seems peaceful.

It's the same with muscle tension. It goes up when stress demands it, but doesn't necessarily come down when the stress is gone. The result is usually chronic headaches, backaches, and nervous tics.

Furthermore, our adaptation to higher stress arousal can occur in response to stressors that we don't even know exist—or at least, don't recognize as stressors. They influence us at the unconscious level, causing our bodies to react with elevated blood pressure or muscle tension, even though we are oblivious to what is causing stress. For instance, any of the following could be causing you stress *right now* without your knowing it:

- driving on busy freeways
- the noise from your teenager's stereo system

- living near noisy freeways or train lines
- loneliness
- complaining neighbors
- bad lighting at work or home
- too much fluorescent lighting
- opening impossibly tight jars
- the neighbors' kids always coming into your garden
- bad time management
- always being late for appointments
- too many deadlines
- a spouse who gives you the silent treatment
- dogs barking in the night

Any or all of these (and I'm sure we can add others to the list) can be the source of subtle, continuous, and potentially ruinous stress, without our even being aware of any discomfort. Our bodies adapt to these circumstances and after a while give us a false sense of well-being by blotting out the discomfort. Eventually we reach pass the point of no return. We are no longer capable of returning to a non-aroused state, and stress disease sets in.

EVEN GOOD THINGS CAN CAUSE BAD STRESS!

No fact I can communicate about stress is more important than this one: even the good things of life can cause bad stress!

The greatest misunderstanding anyone can have about stress is that it is produced only by the unpleasant experiences of life. Many people risk unnecessary stress damage because they believe that only major catastrophes or prolonged conflict produces stress disease. Not true! Most of the men I know (and now increasingly women) who have developed heart disease did not complain of their life circumstances. In fact, they rather enjoyed them!

"Surely stress is only harmful when it is caused by bad things," a patient argued with me after being referred by his physician for stress management training because his blood pressure was too high and his ulcer was bleeding.

"No," I replied, "stress damage can be caused as much by the good things of life as the bad." His puzzlement was amazing to behold. Stress is supposed to come only from bad life experiences. But this is a gross misunderstanding of the body's alarm system.

Jack is another example of someone with this mistaken belief. He is a hard-working, highly driven attorney—tops in his field. He loves his work and savors the thrill of each new challenge. He is happiest when in a crisis that requires him to work intensely and long hours.

If you ask Jack whether he was stressed during one of these crises, he will quickly reply, "No." He's happy, he will say. He's in good shape, he will argue, since he plays handball three times a week. He will say he enjoys his young family and spends time with them. He will insist that there is no stress in his life. But he will be wrong!

Early one morning, shortly after I started seeing him for a headache problem, Jack was awakened by an uncomfortable feeling in his chest. His heart seemed to be skipping beats and he was having difficulty breathing. An intense panic set in. He wondered, "Am I having a heart attack?" He lay there still and quiet for awhile, not wanting to alarm his wife. A half-hour later, he began to feel better and the bad feeling subsided.

The next day Jack called me and I told him to see his internist for a checkup. No, the doctor told him, he wasn't having a heart attack. Yes, he was in good health, except that his blood pressure was up.

"What is wrong, then?" he asked the doctor.

"You are under too much stress." The doctor's words seemed unbelievable to Jack, but hearing those words first from me and then from his physician, he finally accepted the reality of his circumstances.

Jack was experiencing a common variety of panic disorder brought on by the over excitement of his body's stress response system. It is a problem showing a dramatic increase in those with high-pressured jobs, and usually strikes first in the mid to late thirties. Women are perhaps more vulnerable than men. Once a full-blown panic attack has occurred, it may take years to fully recover from it.

Now the point I want to make here is this: panic anxiety disorder often strikes at a time when it seems that everything is going well. It can as easily be caused by doing something pleasurable to excess as by experiencing something painful or unpleasant over a long period of time. The body really can't tell the difference and responds with its defensive actions in exactly the same way.

Dr. Hans Selye, the father of stress research (and originator of the terms *eustress* and *distress* as they are applied to stress), made this clear when he first defined stress as "the nonspecific response of the body to any demand." He emphasizes in all his writings that the body can respond in the same manner to many types of pressure—both good and bad. The excitement of getting married or watching the home team play a winning game can produce as much stress as struggling to meet a publisher's deadline or facing an angry boss. Although the one causes good stress (*eustress*) and the other bad stress (*distress*), both make the same demands on the body and move you away from your normal resting equilibrium. Too much of either type over an extended period of time can work havoc in your body.

Dr. Selye made this discovery many years ago while performing an experiment with laboratory rats that is worth repeating here, if only to prove my point. It vividly shows how all stress— regardless of origin or type—affects the body the same way.

In his early experiments with hormone chemistry, Dr. Selye tried to isolate the effects of individual hormones on laboratory rats. Hormones are the body's chemical messengers, carried through the blood to all the organs. Dr. Selye wanted to find out precisely how different chemicals affected the animal's body. So he injected various prepared substances into a large number of rats.

What Dr. Selye discovered was very confusing at first. He found that no matter what hormone was injected, the internal damage it caused in the rat was always the same. He purified the chemicals extensively, thinking that some impurity was the cause, but saw no difference. Neither did using combinations of hormones. Always, the damage was the same.

Three rather dramatic effects occurred within the bodies of all the animals injected with hormones:

1. The adrenal glands became enlarged to a marked degree, swollen from the demands of stress upon them.

2. The thymus gland, responsible for fighting disease, had atrophied.

3. The animal had developed ulcers.

Dr. Selye puzzled over why different hormones all produced the same results. Then he had one of those "aha" experiences that every researcher dreams about. He realized the experiment was showing that anything which challenges the body's equilibrium will put it into an emergency response mode and, over time, will cause stress damage.

We will see later how this experiment explains many of stress' effects. For now, it will serve to illustrate the crucial point that stress doesn't have to come from unpleasant or negative sources to be bad for us. All excitement and challenge can kill us, no matter its type.

I would even venture to say that the positive, pleasant stressors of life are more likely to lead to stress disease because we don't take steps to avoid them. This is what makes stress disease so mysterious and dangerous.

Of course, a major traumatic life event like divorce or a business failure will contribute its share of damage, but these "big problems" of life are usually time-limited. They are confined to a span of weeks or perhaps months. Sooner or later they pass off the scene. We take steps to get them out of our lives as soon as possible. The other, more challenging or pleasant demands of life can stay with us a long time. Like water dripping on a stone, they eventually wear us down.

In truth, this is only a part of the stress story. But it is a very important part because it is so easy to overlook. While severe physical or emotional distresses can cause significant stress damage, there is a hidden enemy lurking beneath the turbulent waters of every excitement and challenge. By far the greater amount of stress damage today is brought about not by major life traumas, but by agreeable experiences, exciting challenges, or stimulating competition. Until we grasp this central truth, we will never be masters of our stress.

WHAT CAUSES US STRESS?

In summary, let me review the many causes of stress in your life. Stress can result from anything that:

- annoys you
- threatens you
- prods you
- excites you
- scares you
- worries you
- hurries you
- angers you
- frustrates you
- challenges you
- criticizes you
- reduces your self-esteem

Anything—pleasant or unpleasant—that arouses your adrenaline system for too long and mobilizes your body for "fight or flight" predisposes you to stress disease. Your body simply adapts to living in a constant state of emergency—and you feel no discomfort until damaging results occur.

So this is the problem of stress, and I have only begun to tell the story! The real problem is that most people don't realize they've got a problem until it is too late! Or, if they do acknowledge it, they are not sure what to do about it. I hope that as I proceed to unfold the story, you will soon discover ways you can reduce the damage done by stress in your life.

How Stress Does Its Damage

If you clench your fist and place it at the center of your breast-bone, then imagine it is colored pinkish gray and acting like it owned your body, you have just pictured your heart.

The heart is a remarkable organ. It stands at the very core of life, and its beat is central to survival. Believe it or not, every day the heart pumps about two thousand gallons of blood (the equivalent of a hundred large automobile gasoline tanks) through sixty thousand miles of elastic tubing. But the heart is no mere pump!

Dr. Jay Cohn, head of the cardiovascular division of the University of Minnesota Medical School, says, "The heart is actually an incredibly intelligent organ. When you walk up a flight of stairs, when you get nervous or excited, or when someone scares you, your heart immediately responds with changes in rate, force, and contraction."[1] It has this incredible ability to adjust its performance. Even when you transplant a heart, it can go on functioning in another person's chest as if it had always lived there.

It also responds with changes when you become fearful or fall in love! Its rate, force, and contraction all respond with amazing sensitivity to what is needed in the moment. No dumb pump, this is a genius organ of the body around which all life revolves. It can think for itself, thank you.

How does the heart know what to do? It has no direct connection to the nervous system to receive signals from the brain, which is why it can be so easily transplanted. Rather, it is designed to respond to signals from the complex chemical messengers that circulate in the blood—including the adrenaline hormones.

Unfortunately, it is this sensitivity to chemical messengers, the genius of the heart's operations, that carries with it risks as well as advantages. Over a period of time, when out of balance, these same messengers can literally destroy the heart.

THE "HEART" OF THE STRESS PROBLEM

There is one important characteristic of the heart that we should be aware of, therefore, when it comes to understanding how stress damages the body. *The heart, with all its valves, tubing, electrical system, and complex muscles and blood vessels, is the central target of destruction for much of the harmful stress we experience.*

Heart disease is the twentieth century's most serious health problem. An estimated 62.7 million Americans suffer from some form of it. According to the American Heart Association, nearly a million Americans die each year from heart attacks, strokes, and other illnesses related to the cardiovascular system. This is more than all the other causes of death—including cancer, car accidents, and infections put together.

Only seventy or eighty years ago, the risk of heart disease was less, only ranking as the fourth leading cause of death. Having brought many other diseases under control, we now live longer and thus experience a greater risk of heart disease. The older we get, the greater our risk of developing a deteriorating condition of the heart. But this is not the major reason for the increase. The reason is our accelerated pace of life and our failure to control our stress.

In a sense, the greater incidence of heart disease we now experience is a consequence of the many blessings brought by the progress of modern medicine. A longer and more enriching life is a great blessing! But there is no reason at all why we cannot *also* bring heart disease under control. Such control is well within our reach. Low fat diet and the reduction of cigarette smoking are important in our fight against heart disease, but equally, if not more importantly, is our fight against overstress.

CAUSES OF HEART DISEASE

Because heart disease is such an important repercussion of stress in general, we need to pay particular attention to it. Certain risk factors for heart disease are now well known. These include:

- A family history of heart disease and being a male (although females are increasingly at risk).
- Cigarette smoking (stopping smoking can eventually reverse this risk).
- High blood pressure (called the "silent killer" because so many don't know that they have it).
- High blood cholesterol level, especially high levels of the low-density lipoproteins (LDLs) which clog the arteries. (For more on cholesterol, see chapter 7.)

But is this the total picture? Or is it possible that *behind* all these factors is *one* single enemy? I believe it is. As we will see, there is abundant evidence to support the idea that the excessive circulation of the stress hormones, especially *adrenaline*, lies behind all of these other risk factors. This is one reason why cardiovascular problems often run in families. The tendency to run high or become addicted to adrenaline is inherited. It goes with our personality characteristics. If it is not genetic, then it is at least learned at an early age. You either have a predisposition to pump higher levels of adrenaline . . . or you don't.

The most common mechanism underlying the development of heart disease is *atherosclerosis* (from the Greek words for *gruel* and *hardening*), which involves the progressive hardening of the arteries with a build-up of plaque. This disease is thought to begin *early in life* and can be significantly found in about half the population at the time of death.

What is the cause of atherosclerosis? There is still much we don't know, but there is enough evidence to suggest that one of the culprits is the excessive recruitment of adrenaline—the body's emergency hormone.

Most of us live in a highly competitive and demanding life situation. Our exposure begins at an early age and keeps us constantly on the move, striving to outdo others as we reach for greater things. In fact, many of us live our whole lives in what is essentially *a constant state of emergency and hurry.* We become dependent on the overproduction of adrenaline, not simply for our accomplishments, but just to survive each day. The problem with our dependence on high levels of adrenaline is that we have to pay the piper for this abuse later on. What it amounts to is accelerated "wear and tear" on our cardiovascular systems, creating burnout—much like a high performance car that has been allowed to overheat.

This is why the kind of person who is always in a hurry, who has a low tolerance for frustration, and who is highly driven is at such great risk for heart disease. (We will discuss the personality type underlying these tendencies in the next chapter.) This kind of person is known to produce significantly higher levels of circulating adrenaline and related stress hormones. No one can live in a constant state of emergency without paying for it later on with some form of physical disease.

OTHER KINDS OF STRESS DAMAGE

Stress disease is not confined to the heart. It attacks many parts of the body. While the other symptoms of stress are not as life-threatening as heart disease, they certainly have a negative effect on the quality of our lives. Vast numbers of people suffer from debilitating stress symptoms such as headaches, ulcers, digestive problems, or muscle spasms and live very painful and intolerable lives. They depend on medication simply to get them through the day and to help them function at a very basic level. And some will even tell you that living as they do is not much better than being dead!

I strongly feel that too much dependence on medication to alleviate stress symptoms is self-defeating and counterproductive. It is like closing the barn door after the horse has bolted. It mostly treats the symptoms of stress, not the disease. In relieving our symptoms by taking painkillers for our headaches, we make it easy to return to the situation causing the stress rather than avoiding it. Stress symptoms are our allies, warning us of danger and overextension. When we rush in to relieve these symptoms without heeding their warnings, we make it easy to engage in more stress.

How can we become less dependent on drugs for protection against stress disease? How can we reduce or even eliminate the debilitating effects of stress, without taking away the very pain that is there as a protective warning signal or reduce the discomfort meant to warn us of our overstress? I am all in favor of getting as much relief from my stress pain as possible, but it is dangerous for me to refuse to heed my pain's warning signals and fail to back off from my high-stress circumstances!

I believe the gateway to becoming less drug dependent lies in becoming more aware of how the body recruits adrenaline under stress, then finding ways to manage this adrenaline. We can't eliminate our adrenaline, but we can take control of how we recruit it.

UNDERSTANDING THE STRESS RESPONSE

To help the reader understand how the adrenal system works, I have prepared Figure 1. Take a moment to study it. Notice that stress can originate in either external or internal events. While we do experience much of our stress from outside forces we cannot control, much of this outside stress comes from our perception of the world around us. (It is what we think about what is happening to us—our interpretation of the outside world, not just the world itself—that causes us the most stress.) External stressors include threats, adversity, and conflict as well as excitement or challenge.

Other stress originates on the inside. Aloofness, physical handicaps, discomfort, and even depression can produce stress as readily as external threats or life's catastrophes.

I remember once having to undergo surgery . . . nothing major, but still enough to get my attention! For the three or four weeks following the surgery, I monitored my body very closely and

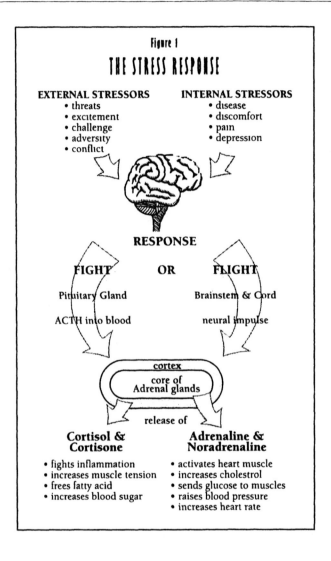

Figure 1

THE STRESS RESPONSE

EXTERNAL STRESSORS
- threats
- excitement
- challenge
- adversity
- conflict

INTERNAL STRESSORS
- disease
- discomfort
- pain
- depression

RESPONSE

FIGHT   OR   FLIGHT

Pituitary Gland   Brainstem & Cord

ACTH into blood   neural impulse

cortex
core of
Adrenal glands

release of

Cortisol &
Cortisone
- fights inflammation
- increases muscle tension
- frees fatty acid
- increases blood sugar

Adrenaline &
Noradrenaline
- activates heart muscle
- increases cholestrol
- sends glucose to muscles
- raises blood pressure
- increases heart rate

discovered that while the surgery wound healed quite well, I
was experiencing many symptoms of stress during the recovery
period. At first, this puzzled me. There were no complications.
Healing was progressing well. Why should I feel as if I were
stressed? Then I realized what was going on in my body. Even
though the process of healing was following its normal course,
the healing process itself was stressful to my body.

The human body doesn't distinguish between whether a stressor is from within or from without the body—it responds the same in either case. What happens is that the brain sends messages along two separate pathways. The first is to the pituitary gland in the brain which releases a substance called adrenocorticotrophic hormone," or ACTH for short. ACTH, in turn, travels rapidly in the blood to stimulate the adrenal glands. (The term *adrenal* literally means "toward kidney," from the Latin *ad renal*. The glands were so named because one adrenal gland is located on top of each kidney.)

The second pathway is through the brain stem and spinal cord, which send nerve impulses to many parts of the body, including the adrenal glands.

The combined effect of these chemical and neural signals is to stimulate the two major parts of the adrenal gland—the "core" and the "cortex." Each part secretes different hormones for differing purposes.

The cortex releases several hormones, but the two most important ones in relation to stress are *cortisol* and *cortisone*, both of which, at normal levels of arousal, help fight pain and inflammation. It is the "core" that releases adrenaline and noradrenaline into the bloodstream. These hormones stimulate the heart, raise the blood pressure, and prepare us for that unique emergency reaction in the body—the "fight, fright, or flight" response. They prepare us physically either to attack the source of our stress or to run away from it. It is as simple as that. The source of stress is seen by the body as an enemy to be fought or avoided.

The effect of this "fight, fright, or flight" response on the rest of the body is extremely important to understand. If we follow this response through its intricate and intertwined pathways, we can readily see how the various symptoms of prolonged stress are created. The process goes something like this:

> The increased demand for blood in the brain (to mobilize us for action) means that the heart has to do *extra* work. The *muscles* (to provide a quick getaway or more force for fighting) and the *stomach* (to digest food and provide needed energy) also demand extra blood,

which then has to be withdrawn from other parts of the body where it is not needed as much. One effect of this need for blood to be shunted to muscles and the stomach during stress is that blood is withdrawn from the hands and feet, the peripheral parts of the body. The reduced circulation of blood in the hands causes the "cold hands" phenomenon so often experienced by those under stress.

Later in this book I will describe a way to monitor your "cold hands" reaction as a way of recognizing when your adrenaline is aroused. The increased activity in the stomach, especially when stress is chronic, often causes ulcers (because of increased acid secretion) and a host of other gastrointestinal complaints. The increased muscle tension causes pain after awhile and is the underlying factor in many headaches and backaches. In Part Two, we will discuss in more detail the wide variety of symptoms that can be brought on by prolonged stress.

But what is important for us to understand here is how the emergency response system of the body can create a state of increased activity *throughout the whole body*—all because the "stress hormones," especially adrenaline, are circulating in large quantities through the bloodstream, carrying their messages of arousal and alertness. Adrenaline is the Paul Revere of the body, heralding the approach of danger!

THE EFFECTS OF ELEVATED ADRENALINE

Besides the mobilizing of our body for fight or flight, the chronic increased flow of adrenaline produces a number of other less helpful and more serious consequences. These include:

- an increase in the production of blood cholesterol
- a narrowing of the capillaries and other blood vessels that can shut down the blood supply to the heart muscle

- a decrease in the body's ability to remove cholesterol
- an increase in the blood's tendency to clot
- an increase in the depositing of plaque on the walls of the arteries.

In short bursts, elevated adrenaline is not damaging or dangerous. In fact, that is what it is designed to do. But when sustained at high levels over a period of time, it can be very harmful. Adrenaline arousal can be compared to revving up a car engine, then leaving it to idle at high speed.

Idling an engine on high for a short period of time clears out gum deposits and dirty carbon. It is good for an engine. But when the engine is left idling for a long time, carbon deposits begin to collect in the valves and the engine not only becomes gunked up, it wears out faster. Carbon is an abrasive that damages surfaces.

This is more or less what happens in the heart during prolonged and chronic elevation of adrenaline. The adrenaline keeps the system moving at a high speed, and deterioration occurs at a faster rate. We actually age faster.

Why, then, don't we naturally recognize the danger of stress, especially the stress of challenging activities, and stop our destructive behavior? The answer is quite simply this: since elevated adrenaline can also give us a heightened sense of well-being, increased energy, reduced need for sleep, and feelings of excitement or even euphoria, we falsely think that high adrenaline is good for us. This is why it is so addicting. We are completely unaware of its hidden dangers. It is easy to see why many become addicted to a state of high arousal. The feelings of security it provides can give us a dangerously false sense of well-being.

Because it is vital to the rest of this book, let me once more emphasize this most critical fact: The most serious effect of elevated adrenaline, when persistent and unrelenting, is its damage to the heart and arteries. Drs. Meyer Friedman and Ray Rosenman, the cardiologists who first identified the personality type most prone to heart disease, clearly prove from their research the connection between prolonged adrenaline arousal and heart disease. They state:

"The chronic excess discharge and circulation of the catecholamines (adrenaline and noradrenaline) . . . may be the chief factor in the total process of arterial decay and thrombosis. We have seen coronary heart disease erupt in many subjects whose blood insulin levels and metabolism of cholesterol, fat, and sugar were quite normal. But rarely have we ever witnessed the onset of this disease in a person whose rate of manufacture and secretion of catecholamines (adrenaline and noradrenaline) we did not know or suspect to have been increased."[2]

LEARNING TO LIVE ON LESS ADRENALINE

What does all this mean? Simply this: To avoid cardiovascular disease and other stress-related disorders, it is not enough to eat the right food and keep cholesterol levels low. This is important, BUT IT IS NOT ENOUGH! It is not enough to exercise regularly and even to take regular vacations. To protect yourself against dying of or suffering ill effects from stress, you must learn how to switch off your production of adrenaline when it is no longer needed, and stop using it for non-emergency life situations (like driving on the freeway)! We've got to become less dependent on this emergency hormone for everyday living.

Since anger, frustration, irritation, challenge, and excitement are all adrenaline triggers (they depend on high adrenaline to do their thing), these psychological triggers must also be brought under our conscious control. Effective stress management requires that we be healthy in mind and spirit, not just in our bodies. This is what I mean by "adrenaline management." It means controlling the problem at its source. It means cutting off the stress that wastes adrenaline.

How does this translate into practical, everyday advice? If you love excitement and enjoy the thrill of a challenge, you will have to work a little harder at controlling your adrenaline. You have a greater tendency to produce too much adrenaline. If you thrive on novelty and change, you may have to work at learning to enjoy life without a flow of novel stimulation. If you don't know how to relax, you will have to train yourself to come down frequently from the "mountaintop" and enjoy the peace of the valley, where recuperation and healing can take place. In later chapters of this book, I will provide some specific and practical suggestions for how to do this.

The accelerated pace of modern living tends to rob us of natural recovery time. We have shortened the night with the invention of electricity and robbed ourselves of the natural recovery time provided by horse travel. To deal with stress, we need to find equivalent "rest" times throughout our day. If we don't design it into our lifestyles, it won't happen. Just as we are conscious of time in our fast-track careers, so we need to develop a consciousness for our need for rest. The Bible has a lot to say about the Sabbath, the day of rest. What has always fascinated me about the laws governing Sabbath keeping in the old covenant is that the penalty for breaking the laws was *death by stoning*. Wasn't that a rather severe penalty for failure to observe a day most of us take for granted today? Not really. The truth is that even today the penalty for not taking time to slow down and give our bodies adequate rest is *still death*. Only it is a slow, self-inflicted death . . . death caused by too much stress!

Stress as "Hurry Sickness"

I have a friend about my age who is also a psychologist. He lives in another part of the country, so I don't get to see him often. What makes this friend very special is that he is almost a mirror image of me, and I don't mean that we look alike! He's more handsome and athletic than I am. No, I mean that we tend to behave very much alike. And because of this we understand each other very well. He gets angry at the same things I do. He becomes impatient in the same kinds of situations that make me impatient. And he becomes restless when he has nothing to do—just like me! Eerie!

What we have in common is known as a "Type-A personality." Or, more accurately, the "Type-A coronary disease-prone personality."

My friend suffered a severe heart attack some years ago. He survived the attack, but has never been the same since. He is much *better!* He has learned to be more attentive to his personal needs. Also, he is becoming more patient, more loving, and even more spiritual, although he has never been a very religious person. And because I can identify with my friend so closely, his heart attack has helped me to become a lot more level-headed also.

THE TYPE-A PERSONALITY

The idea that there is a particular type of personality that is more prone to experience distress is now widely accepted although, of course, it must be recognized that not everybody can be put into a simple two-box category. In fact, most people are really a mixture of many characteristics. But for our purposes, it can be helpful to think of ourselves as fitting into one category or the other. No doubt you have heard many references to these personality categories—"Type A" and "Type B" (with those people who seem to have an even mixture of the two being labeled "Type X"). Sometimes such a category is called "Type A (or B) *Personality;* at other times it is referred to as "Type-A (or B) *Behavior Pattern,* or simply TABP (or TBBP).

I should also say at this point that some researchers do take issue with this simple classification system. For example, H. J. Eysenk, a British psychologist, believes that Type-A qualities such as tenseness, ambition, and activity are found in varying degrees in all of us. But again, the important thing at this point is not putting people in categories but understanding how stress affects us and having some way of telling whether we lean strongly or weakly in the direction of trouble.

In my experience, the tool of personality categorization has been very helpful. What are the traits displayed by those who are predominately Type A? Type-A behavior is an "action-emotion complex" that can be seen in those persons who are always struggling to achieve more and more in less and less time. In essence, they are always in a hurry. Of course, there are other characteristics that describe the Type-A person as well:

- They have a high degree of competitiveness.
- They are easily irritated by delays.
- They have a low tolerance for frustration.
- They are hard-driving and ambitious.
- They are highly aggressive.
- They are easily angered and often have free-floating hostility.

- They cannot relax without feeling guilty.
- They are confident on the surface but insecure within.
- They speak aggressively, accentuating key words.
- They have a tendency to finish other people's sentences.

What percentage of the population is Type A? This is a hard question to answer. Estimates range from 50 percent to 70 percent, depending on how personality types are measured and whether the population being studied is urban or rural. Type B's seem to be less prominent in our large cities, presumably because that is where Type-A qualities are most reinforced!

I experience my Type-A pattern quite readily whenever I go to the supermarket. I usually go for a long bicycle ride in the evening. When I do, my wife asks me to stop at the supermarket and buy a few things. After I've loaded the shopping basket with the milk, fruit, bread, and other essentials, I go to the "express lane" checkout. The sign says "CASH ONLY—NO MORE THAN TWELVE ITEMS." I stand there looking at the people ahead of me and begin to fume. I count the items in their baskets. (Woe betide anyone who exceeds twelve items.) Restlessly, I ask myself, *Why is this express line the slowest of all?* I look at the regular checkout lines. They always seem to be going faster. Finally my turn comes, and with a great sense of relief I leave the supermarket resolving never to be frustrated again—until I return the next evening!

Type-B people, on the other hand, are relatively free of most of the habits I have described above. They do not feel bound by time, have less sense of urgency, and find time to play and relax. They are patient, slow to anger, and less concerned about what peers and superiors may think about their actions. They have resigned themselves to the restrictions that their humanness places upon them.

Type B's may appear to be the "tortoises" of our world alongside the Type-A "rabbits," but this isn't altogether a fair analogy. Many Type B's are high achievers and are in positions of responsibility. They are energetic and fast when the task demands it, but they can "switch off" and take it easy when the crisis is over.

Figure 2

TYPE-A BEHAVIOR PATTERN TEST

Read each question carefully and give yourself a score according to the following descriptions:

Score   Description

0   This statement does not apply to me.
1   It sometimes applies to me (less than once a month).
2   It often applies to me (more than once a month).

Statement   **Score**

1. I feel like there isn't enough time in each day
    to do all the things I need to do.   _____

2. I tend to speak faster than other people, even
    finishing their sentences for them.   _____

3. My spouse or friends say, or I believe, that I
    eat too quickly.   _____

4. I would rather win than lose a game.   _____

5. I am very competitive in work, sports, or
    games.   _____

6. I tend to be bossy and dominate others.   _____

7. I prefer to lead rather than follow.   _____

8. I feel pressed for time even when I am not
    doing something important.   _____

9. I become impatient when I have to wait for
    something or when I am interrupted.   _____

10. I tend to make decisions quickly, even
    impulsively.   _____

11. I take on more than I can accomplish.   _____

12. I become irritable (and even angry) more
    often than most other people.   _____

                                          Total Score   _____

ANALYZING YOUR SCORE

- If your total score is less than 5, you are definitely not a Type-A person. You may occasionally slip into Type-A behavior, but not often enough for it to be a problem.

- From 6 to 10, you are beginning to show occasional signs of Type-A behavior. You may have a temporary irritation in your life or some aspect of your work is getting to you. You are approaching the Type-A behavior pattern as you get nearer the upper end of this score. You may be a mixture of Type A and Type B.

- From 11 to 16, you are definitely a Type-A person. At the higher end of this score, you are becoming prone to excessive adrenaline recruitment and are likely to be evidencing signs of distress.

- Above 17, not only are you a Type-A person but you are living dangerously. Life may be miserable for you but it can also be very exciting. Either way, you are prone to develop cardiovascular deterioration if you do not change your behavior pattern. If you smoke or have any of the other high-risk factors (diabetes, high blood pressure, or family history of heart disease), I advise you to seek professional help.

Of course, no person is a pure Type A or Type B. Most of us are a blend of the two. But this categorization helps to point up our predominating characteristics.

Figure 2 presents a brief test for the Type-A personality style so that you can determine what your predominant personality type is. The key for interpreting your score is found in Appendix at the end of this book.

THE PENALTY FOR TYPE-A TENDENCIES

There are some good things about being a Type-A person. People with this personality type accomplish a lot. They get things done. And often their sense of hurry comes from caring deeply about and feeling responsible for the world around them.

But there is a physical penalty to be paid for being a predominantly Type-A person. Type-A people recruit very much more adrenaline than Type B. And research has shown that Type-A men have *three times* the incidence of heart disease as Type-B men. This is rapidly becoming true of women, also, as they move into more competitive lifestyles. Whereas a higher percentage of women used to be considered Type B, now the dominant type in women is rapidly becoming Type A. And with this change has come a dramatic increase in heart disease among women.

What is important to remember is that the stress hormones, including adrenaline, are *always found in excessive amounts* in these individuals. Type-A behavior patterns and higher levels of adrenaline are lifelong partners. Whether you pump high adrenaline *because* you are Type A, or you pump high adrenaline and this *makes* you Type A isn't clear. It's a typical chicken-and-egg dilemma!

Since the Type A and Type B descriptions of personality have been well discussed in other books on stress, it is not my intention to focus on these personality traits in depth here. In this chapter, I want to focus on the *one characteristic of the Type-A behavior pattern* that I believe to be the most neglected and therefore the most dangerous of all—*the sense of time urgency* that gives rise to what I call "hurry sickness." And I want to look at the ways this time urgency has permeated the lives of us all, creating what could be termed a "Type-A culture." So it is important to understand what "Type-A-ness" is about—even if you are more Type B. Doing so can help you withstand the pressures you feel around you, pushing you to become Type A. It's not all its cracked up to be!

"HURRY SICKNESS"—A TWENTIETH-CENTURY DISEASE

A large part of the damage we experience in our lives is caused by "hurry sickness." It comes from our urge to live and do everything in haste. As a consequence, we live at a pace too fast for our bodies. This hurried lifestyle creates a persistent *internal state of emergency* that keeps our stress hormones elevated.

At least 50 percent—probably more—of the characteristics of the Type-A behavior pattern can be accounted for by the notion of "hurriedness." Type-A persons constantly struggle against time.

They hate to "waste time" eating, having a haircut, or sitting in the park. They hate waiting in line and are always active, restless, moving, doing things. And Type-A people pay for their sense of time urgency in increased circulation of adrenaline and consequent stress damage.

But there's another aspect to hurry sickness that transcends basic tendencies and personality types. Hurriedness has become a distinguishing characteristic of the age we live in. Life has quite literally "speeded up." One of the culprits is technology. Social critic Jeremy Rifkin believes that what has changed is our perception of time itself. The computer age has introduced to our society a segment of time called the *nanosecond*. A nanosecond is a *billionth* of a second—a measurement of time so minuscule that it is impossible to conceive. We can certainly never experience it because the nanosecond is faster than our own nervous systems can chart. Such a tiny particle of time is beyond our consciousness and vanishes before we can know it! But the warp-speed world of computers is having an impact on our own life-pace. Normal human interaction—the speed at which we think and talk, the level of urgency we bring to shopping or just relaxing—is steadily getting faster. A recent report cited children complaining that their teachers talk too slowly, when compared with Nintendo. XT computers, once hailed as fantastically fast, are now rejects because they make us wait a second longer than Pentiums. I know. Every time I upgrade one of my several computers, I lose patience with my old, outdated one.

Type A's and Type B's alike are coming under the influence of a technologically accelerating world. They are constantly being bombarded by demands to do more and more . . . faster and faster. Expanded opportunities and enhanced communication also mean constant stimulation and demand. My office computer E-mail system, now connected to all my faculty . . . and beyond, means that I have to immediately respond to all mail—and there is more of it, simply because it is easier to generate. And while Type A's probably get caught up more strongly in this feature of our changing culture, none of us is immune to it.

This raises an interesting question. Have humans always suffered from hurry sickness? I teach many stress management seminars to ministers and missionaries. One of the questions most frequently asked is, "Why were great preachers like John Wesley and Charles Spurgeon not bothered by stress disease? They worked long hours, gave of themselves unselfishly, and sacrificed many luxuries. Yet they seemed to be free of what bothers us."

(Actually, Spurgeon suffered from deep depressions, but the question is still a valid one.)

My answer is usually quite simple: These men lived in a different age. Hurry sickness is largely a phenomenon of the twentieth century. It began with the industrial revolution and has continued to increase right up to the present. In previous times, travel was slow and allowed much time for reflection and recuperation. We no longer have the luxury of time, much to our regret.

The pace of life has accelerated dramatically in the past forty or fifty years. Most of us barely find time to brush our teeth, let alone spend time in relaxation, meditation, or reflection. Our culture is oriented toward speed and efficiency; it is hard to succeed unless we keep up with or move faster than everyone else. And I am as guilty of being caught up in this rat race as anyone.

Consider for a moment what life was like in previous times. A few thousand years ago, the fastest mode of travel for most people was on foot, or perhaps on the backs of donkeys or camels—at the speed of about four or five miles an hour. A chariot could race between cities at the fantastic pace of about twenty miles an hour, but only a few could enjoy this luxury. Today, however, we can all travel at quite amazing speeds in automobiles and airplanes. No doubt we'll be able to speed up normal transportation even further with the advent of bullet trains and underground zip tubes.

Gone is the leisurely, slow-paced way of life that once existed. We no longer have much time for contemplation—or more important—time to allow our bodies to relax so that restoration and healing can take place. In past times, without electricity, evenings were calm and unstimulated, allowing the adrenaline system to "switch off." But today there is hardly a moment when we are not bombarded with stimuli—from the moment we wake up until, exhausted, we switch off late-night television. The toll our fast-paced lives takes on our adrenal systems is quite frightening—and mostly unrecognized.

In Bible times, oil was expensive. When the sun went down, the day stopped for everyone. Nighttime was for resting and this allowed adequate recovery for people's bodies. This, coupled with plenty of physical outlets, ensured that stress was not the threat to health and happiness that it is today. (True, people died young in Bible times because of disease and poor sanitary conditions, but they didn't die from stress disease.)

I grew up in Southern Africa and know something of life in a more primitive culture. African culture has always fascinated me because, in many respects, it has taught me a number of important lessons about my preoccupation with time. It has helped me, for instance, to put my Western culture in proper perspective and has pointed the way to a more balanced life.

For Westerners, most Africans' indifference to time is maddening. Church seldom starts on time. They go on for hours and hours and certainly never stop when they are supposed to. Why should they? The world's not going anywhere! Africans are just not hooked on time. In earlier times, when clocks first came to the continent, Africans thought clocks and wrist watches caused time to pass, not measure it. So they avoided clocks and watches entirely.

My digital wrist watch, the most modern available, can tell me what time it is—up to a hundredth of a second. Most Africans can tell time by the sun to the nearest hour. I suffer from being under a lot of stress. They seldom do. Sometimes I almost wish I could trade my Seiko for a sundial . . . almost!

About a year ago I was scheduled to speak at a conference in Chicago. I went to my office on a Friday morning, saw three patients, drove to Los Angeles International Airport, flew to Chicago, and got there in time to address an evening meeting. I spoke three times on Saturday and twice on Sunday, then flew back to Los Angeles in time to get to bed. The next morning I went to work as usual.

Such hectic, "rush about" activity takes a heavy stress toll on one's body. And needless to say, four days later I came down with a severe influenza attack—attributable, I believe, to a case of overextension and overstress. My immune system had simply given out.

You see, the human body is designed for camel travel, but we keep driving it as if it were a supersonic jet. Camel travel allows plenty of time for rest and recovery. Supersonic travel keeps us tense and stressed and allows no time for the rejuvenation that our delicate physical systems need to survive.

Now, I am not saying that we should give up jets or many other conveniences that help us to be more effective and efficient. I thank God for jets every day I travel. But I am saying that we need to recognize that the human frame has its limits, and that we should build into our lives adequate rest and recovery time so as to allow for healing and restoration to take place.

This is the problem: People in a hurry don't allow time for their complex bodies and minds to become revitalized. So they accelerate the wear and tear of their bodies. There is no time for contemplation or even meditation. Anxiety increases and they lose perspective on their problems because they don't have time to think constructively. This makes them even more stressed and less able to cope with the strains of life, thus exacerbating the stress.

In short, people of our time are showing signs of physiological and psychological disintegration because they are living at warp speed. The pace of modern life is too fast for average human bodies, and stress disease is the manifestation of the deterioration that follows the abuse of the body and mind. This is the essence of the stress problem facing us today.

Not only do most of us live life in the fast lane where there is little time for real rest, but social and moral values are changing so rapidly that trying to remain in harmony with our being is itself becoming more and more stressful. My daughters often remind me how much pressure they get from peers to "go with the crowd" or to throw away the values we've tried to inculcate in them. Choosing to be "good" can be very tough going in today's world.

And our lives are changing in other ways that keep our stress levels high. For one thing, we are becoming a more and more mobile society. It is estimated that the average adult makes six job-related moves during a lifetime. And each move is a major upheaval involved in buying or renting a home, changing schools for the children, adjusting to new friends, finding new physicians, locating a new church or synagogue.

These changes and others like them can be so stressful that some researchers point to "life change"—both positive and negative—as a significant measurement of how much stress a person is undergoing.

After studying many patients who had undergone life change ranging from minor to significant, Drs. Tom Holmes and Richard Rahe developed a scale to measure the stress value of these events by assigning corresponding point values to each of them. Holmes and Rahe then followed their subjects' progress for two years and found that anyone undergoing significant life change became more prone to becoming ill. The greater the number and severity of changes (as indicated by a high "score" on the scale), the greater the risk for illness.

Now, we have always known that a lot of stress can make you sick. But what is significant about the Holmes and Rahe research is that they discovered that it didn't matter whether the life change was good or bad; both made people more prone to sickness. You see, it was the *change* that caused the stress. And even good change, like getting married, taking a trip, or even birthdays or Christmas time, impacted stress levels and lowered their immune systems.

Change demands adjustment, and adjustment causes adrenaline arousal. Our complex and hurried lives, with its many and frequent demands for change, can significantly increase our susceptibility to stress damage.

TURNING BAD STRESS INTO GOOD STRESS

It would be unfair for me to suggest that all challenge, change, excitement, and fervor for work or play is bad and should be avoided. True, it is stressful—but it is not my intention to paint change as all bad, nor would it be a completely accurate picture.

Life is to be lived—and lived to the fullest. To be highly motivated to accomplish some task and able to work with enthusiasm is a great blessing. To experience the flood of energy that propels one into action to meet a deadline or accomplish a demanding task is what makes life worthwhile. Just try living without it and see how miserable life can be! Without such challenges, we might as well be dead. Progress in medicine would slow to a snail's pace, justice for the oppressed would never get a helping hand, and even our children would languish from no direction or encouragement.

Nothing worthwhile can be accomplished without some arousal of the stress response system. It is a biological law that we must work, and even fight, to accomplish a worthwhile goal. Challenge and fulfillment are important to health and well being. The lack of it causes us to atrophy in body and mind. But—and this point is crucial to my whole argument—challenge and stress must be accompanied by, and work in harmony with, *relaxation and rest.*

This raises a very important question. Is there really such a thing as "good" stress? In chapter 1, I tried to differentiate between harmful *distress* and helpful, healthy *eustress.* But here we encounter a problem, because we also see from the Holmes and Rahe research that *any stress,* good or bad, causes the body to undergo virtually the same reaction.

What, then, makes the difference between good and bad stress? There are two important answers:

- *Eustress* (healthy stress) results when we adapt to our stressors and successfully cope with them.

- *Eustress* results when we quickly bring our systems back to a state of rest and low arousal.

To tell the truth, I am almost afraid to concede that there is such a thing as good stress, for fear that doing so might perpetuate excuses and rationalizations to continue living over-hurried lives. Too many hide behind the belief that "some pressure is good for us" and explain away their hectic and hurried lives with: "But I *enjoy* what I do—so it can't be all that bad," or "But I *don't feel anxious or tense,* so I can't be under all that much stress."

This is a delusion. I have known quite a few people who have died from heart attacks. And most of them enjoyed, up to the last minute of their lives, the process that led to the destruction of their cardiovascular systems. None of them complained. On the contrary, they objected to anyone intruding into their denial by reminding them that they might be more stressed than they realized. Remember, adrenal arousal is seldom unpleasant; it invigorates and excites while it wears our systems down. This is why it is necessary to emphasize over and over the importance of rest in avoiding stress damage. Bad stress can become good *only* if we bring ourselves back to a state of tranquillity as soon as possible. Good stress must have this pattern about it on an hourly, daily, and weekly basis: High adrenaline arousal can be allowed when demanded, but then the adrenal system must be brought back to a state of low arousal afterward.

The pattern should look like a series of hills and valleys. Every mountain of high arousal should be followed by a valley of recuperation. Each day should end with a return to low arousal. Each challenge of the day should end with a calming of the body. And each week of work should end with rest. If you can do this, you will be healthy in body, mind, and spirit—and all your stress will be "good." You will be obedient to nature's laws for your total person, and this will bring you health.

Whatever we may believe theologically about the Sabbath as was instituted under the Old Covenant, the benefits to be derived from a strict observance of it are tremendous in terms of stress protection and the turning of bad stress into good stress. I don't mean to turn all religious on you at this point, but most modern-day religious people, especially Christians like myself, work harder on their day of worship than they do on regular work days. They have countless activities planned, and many church services are designed toward *stimulation and excitement* rather than *prayer and meditation*. Adrenaline flows as strongly during these worshipful times as it does during a hectic business meeting or a day spent complying with a myriad of demands.

Let me repeat once again: *We all need some stress* to keep us functioning at our maximum effectiveness and to do worthwhile things in our world. Even a high-powered sports car needs to be taken out occasionally and run to the maximum to keep it in good shape. But too much stress or, to stick with my analogy, running the sports car at full throttle continuously, is harmful.

The key word is *balance*, with lots of relaxation thrown in for good measure.

THE ANTIDOTE FOR "HURRY SICKNESS"

"Hurry sickness" is a killer of innocent people—people who don't know that the disease does its damage insidiously and right before their eyes. In their haste they are oblivious to it and even encourage it through ignorance.

Our culture, especially for those of us who fit the Type-A personality profile, tends to have a warped perspective about time. On one hand, we think of it as the "enemy," so we're always trying to "beat the clock" as if time were against us. On the other hand, we almost seem to worship time. We place big clocks on tall steeples where we can all stare at them, then attach large bells that can clang out the hours to remind us how little we are accomplishing.

There was an era when the reminder of the passage of time was helpful in slowing us down. "There's lots of time," I can remember my grandfather saying as the big clock in the hall chimed ten in the morning. "Let's take a break and go fishing down at the river." These days my digital wrist watch beeps to remind me that the hour is up, so I have to say to a patient, "Time is gone; I need to hurry on to my next client." And my stomach doesn't feel quite the same as it did when my grandfather's clock did the chiming.

From time to time, we have all experienced that feeling of renewal that comes from a period of real rest. Perhaps a vacation—or even a forced illness—slowed us down and we found a new sense of inner peace. Freed from deadlines, demands, and conflicts, we "let down" and even discovered a new inner self or some resiliency we never knew we had.

A few years ago I enjoyed one of the privileges given to those in academia—a sabbatical year. Times are changing, however, so I don't know how much longer sabbaticals are going to be around. I'm due for one shortly, so I hope I make it!

Free of regular duties, I could devote myself to reading, study, writing, and in-depth conversations. My wife attests to the fact that after the third month of that sabbatical, I was a different person. Free of any race with time, I seemed more at peace. I discovered some new sensations I never knew and rediscovered some I had forgotten. I became more alert and attentive to the world around me. I even got to know our neighbors. When I came to the end of my sabbatical, one big question hung in my mind. Was I going to go back to being my old self? Would "hurry sickness" invade my soul again and dominate my lifestyle? Would I go back to gulping down my food, talking rapidly, and ignoring the birds in my garden? I resolved I wouldn't let it happen, and by and large, my wife says that in the years since that first, and only, sabbatical I have been different. My attitude toward delays has changed; my reaction to frustrating people has mellowed; and I am able to control my sense of urgency rather than letting it control me. I feel more efficient, my thinking is clearer, and I am content with my accomplishments. Sometimes I speed up to meet a deadline, but mostly I try to savor every morsel of time. I can't wait to see what this next sabbatical will do for me. I anticipate that I will be making some major life changes as I move into the final decade of my working life!

Once more, let me reiterate that I am not advocating that we disengage from life and ignore its challenges. I am also not suggesting that we give up the race for success and retreat to a state of non-achievement. What I am emphasizing is that right in the middle of our hectic, hurried lives we need to learn how to slow down when necessary and find time for relaxation and rest. I'll have a lot more to say about this topic later.

One great lesson I am learning is that the way we travel through life is ours to choose. Whether we travel in the city and on busy freeways, or in the country or desert on unkempt roads, it is easier to achieve the right balance when we are not hurrying than when we chase the wind. To be caught up with the demands of modern-day life without ever slowing down is disastrous. Hitting each day at supersonic speed without ever taking time to slow down will burn out our body engines.

Stress and Anxiety

Stress and anxiety go together like Jack and Jill. You never see one without the other! No discussion about stress would be complete without some comments about how stress and anxiety are tied together. Anxiety is such a common problem that you encounter it almost everywhere. As many as forty million Americans suffer from incapacitating anxiety that lasts long enough, is severe enough, and causes sufficient agony as to make life not worth living.

One form of anxiety, called *panic anxiety disorder*, is the most frightening of all and is showing a dramatic increase in recent years, especially among women.

THE STRONGEST ARE MOST VULNERABLE

As we will see, it is the panic form of anxiety that is most linked to stress as a cause. And the sufferers of panic anxiety are not the weakest among us. Usually there has been no previous sign of anxious tendency. The attacks come on suddenly after years of successful living—but also high-stress living. Many have succumbed to it, believing they were impervious to the inroads of stress. They have pushed themselves too far and panic disorder is the piper they must pay.

Sometimes the distress is so devastating that all these sufferers can do is watch helplessly as their careers and families fall apart.

And then they add to their misery the profound sense of inadequacy or guilt. "If only I were stronger, I could have avoided this," one client, a top business executive, once said to me. "This problem must be a sign that I am totally hopeless." It took a lot of influence on my part to convince him that it was not his uselessness or personal inadequacy that caused his "breakdown," but his ignorance of basic physiology and failure to acknowledge his limits.

There's not much you can do about personal imperfections, but a lot you can do about ignorance!

Most strong people who suffer from stress-induced panic attacks tend to feel so embarrassed about their condition that they refuse to seek treatment or seek it too late. For them, what could be a reversible condition becomes a lifelong handicap.

Since panic anxiety disorder can be prevented, even in those persons with a strong predisposition, it is important to know how stress causes the problem as well as how to self-diagnose the condition in its early stages.

It is also important not to see the problem as a purely psychological one. Our culture tends to stigmatize "emotional" problems without justification. Here, however, we are not dealing with an emotional problem as such, but a complex biological one that has severe emotional consequences. This is the *good news* I bring for most anxiety sufferers: your anxiety problems are not just in your head. They are both real and treatable. So if anxiety is a problem for you, stop blaming yourself or writing yourself off as "weak." Even if treatment has failed for you, take heart! That failure may just mean that you haven't yet discovered the real cause for your anxiety. Exciting new discoveries are being made all the time, and our skill in applying these discoveries grows steadily.

THE LINK BETWEEN ANXIETY AND STRESS

The mechanisms linking stress and anxiety are not perfectly understood, but enough is known to pinpoint overstress as a significant causal factor, especially in panic anxiety attacks. Understanding the link between stress and anxiety can help us, therefore, in preventing a lot of human misery caused by these common disorders.

How does stress cause an increase in anxiety? There are at least two mechanisms we know of, and possibly others as well, that upset the fine balance of natural tranquilizers in the brain. I will confine my discussion to these two. The first is the direct impact of stress on these tranquilizers and the second is an indirect effect.

But first, let me explain how and why it is that we remain tranquil most of the time. The reason why we are able to remain calm and peaceful is that the brain has its own fantastic chemical factory that produces hormones that keep us tranquil and pain free. There are *receptors* in the brain that receive these hormones and respond to their signals, very much like a lock receives a key and opens in response to the right pattern of the key. When the natural tranquilizing hormone is present, the receptor shuts off its signals, producing tranquillity or pain relief.

Now to the *first* of the two mechanisms that cause anxiety. As stress levels rise and become protracted, the brain increases its natural tranquilizers and painkillers to protect us during the *fight or flight* emergency. After awhile, as the stress continues, it begins to close the supply down.

Why does it do this? In a sense, there is a natural protective system at work. Both our pain and our anxiety increase as stress is prolonged, as a way of telling us to *quit* doing that which damages us. If our bodies didn't do this, we would self-destruct. It would mean that the more stress we create, the more peaceful we would feel. This wouldn't be very helpful at all. It would encourage us to seek out more and more stress, thus perpetuating the cycle until we drop! Nature is not stupid! These mechanisms are designed for our protection, not our destruction.

So, the next time you begin to feel more pain or your mind begins to drive you crazy with worry, don't complain—just be thankful for your wonderful body and heed the warning that both your pain and anxiety is sending you.

The *second* mechanism worth knowing about concerns another stress hormone called "cortisol," which is also produced by the adrenal glands and, in fact, is produced in almost direct proportion to adrenaline—the one aids the other.

However, the cortisol that is a problem for anxiety comes from within the brain itself. Some interesting research, first done in Australia, shows that under stress, cortisol production goes up in the brain to such an extent that it forms a barrier to the brain's natural tranquilizers, thus blocking them from reaching their receptors. The result? High anxiety, especially panic anxiety attacks.

Panic anxiety, therefore, is a very common consequence of overstress. It is becoming an increasingly serious and common problem. It is one of the most common emotional problems seen in women.

Why is it more common in women today? I believe it is because women are generally under more stress these days. They often have to work outside the home as well as take care of their families, and most single-family homes are headed by women—with high-stress consequences.

RECOGNIZING ANXIETY SYMPTOMS

There are two steps to developing your ability to recognize anxiety. The *first* is to increase your awareness of when anxiety is present and to differentiate it from other emotional problems such as depression. The *second* is to pinpoint the particular form of the anxiety you are experiencing so that the appropriate treatment can be applied.

Recognizing anxiety is easier if the signs or symptoms are separated into their three categories: physiological, behavioral, and emotional. The symptoms of different forms of anxiety tend to be concentrated in one of these different categories. The list of symptoms is very long, but the following are the most important:

Physical Symptoms

Headaches, dizziness, insomnia, fatigue, trembling, dry mouth, vague aches and pains, excessive perspiration, heartburn, ringing in the ears, flushing, pounding heart, tense muscles, and palpitations.

BEHAVIORAL SYMPTOMS

Lack of concentration, loss of memory, compulsive behavior, restlessness, fidgetiness, lack of motivation, and irritability.

EMOTIONAL SYMPTOMS

Fear of dying, worry, tearfulness, nervousness, morbid self-awareness, increased guilt or shame, fear of "going crazy," panic feelings, and fear of impending doom.

HOW TO INTERPRET THE SYMPTOMS

Now, before you rush out to persuade your doctor to prescribe a tranquilizer for your supposed anxiety problem, let me caution you not to over-interpret this long list of symptoms. Obviously, we all have times when we experience some form of anxiety, along with many of these symptoms. It is only when these symptoms become severe or incapacitating that they constitute a serious anxiety problem.

Take dizziness, for example. Dizziness is often a symptom of anxiety. But you may also feel dizzy due to an inner ear infection, lack of sleep, medication, or even car travel. Dizziness alone is not an unmistakable sign of anxiety. In fact, no single symptom is. Anxiety symptoms should be looked at in their totality.

In determining whether or not you have a problem with anxiety, you must take into account three variables:

1. The *number* of symptoms you recognize (and whether or not they can be attributed to other causes).

2. The *length of time* you have experienced the symptoms.

3. Their *intensity*.

If you have experienced several of these symptoms for a long period of time, and no other physical cause has been identified, then you may be justified in suspecting an anxiety problem, especially if you have been under stress for a while.

The *intensity* of your symptoms is an especially important consideration. The more intense the symptom, the more likely it is to be significant. Intense symptoms, such as those that make it difficult for you to carry out your regular duties, may require treatment even if the source proves to be something other than anxiety.

One of the unfortunate characteristics of anxiety is that it can severely accentuate negative feelings about itself. Being anxious makes your *fear* about being anxious worse—if you follow me! Anxiety feeds on itself in a self-defeating way, so don't hesitate to get professional help if you feel it getting out of control.

PRISONERS OF PANIC ANXIETY

While there are many forms of anxiety—including separation anxiety, phobias, worry anxiety, and free-floating anxiety, just to mention a few—one type of anxiety will generally predominate in those who are under high stress: *panic anxiety*. In its early stages, it may only be a mild feeling of panic. Later it can be so fear-provoking that even robust people are brought to their knees in fear of it.

Of all the anxiety disorders, panic attacks have received the most attention. This is partly because they are the easiest of the anxiety disorders to understand—their symptoms are more or less consistent from person to person, (and even from culture to culture). This is partly because they are so common. Their incidence increases dramatically each year. Recent research by the National Institute of Mental Health shows that in North America, anxiety disorders of the panic variety are the number one mental health problem among women today and second only to drug and alcohol abuse among men.

Some four to ten million Americans, mostly women in the childbearing years, experience panic attacks every year. And they are mostly high achievers—highly educated and very competent people. They have histories of strong personalities, above average abilities, and usually a high tolerance for stress—until the first attack of panic.

Peter's experience is typical and helps illustrate the symptoms of a panic attack. At twenty-eight years of age, he had gone back to university to complete an advanced degree in engineering. One fine spring day he sat down to take an examination with other students. Little did he realize how that day would change the course of his life.

Just as he was nearing completion of the examination, which up to that point was going well for him, Peter felt a sudden surge of fear. He described it this way:

> "For no apparent reason, and right out of the blue, I felt overwhelmed by an intense panic feeling. Something very bad, very evil, was going to happen. A feeling of doom came over me. My heart started to race. I could hardly breathe; it felt like someone was shutting off the air to my lungs. My chest felt tight, like a steel band was around it. I got scared. Man, did I get scared! I started to sweat profusely. My hands trembled uncontrollably and my heart felt it was going to explode."

Peter got up and left the examination room, found a bench nearby, and collapsed onto it. A passing student found him, helped Peter to his car, and took him to the hospital, fearing he was having a heart attack.

After a thorough physical evaluation Peter was sent home; there was nothing wrong with his heart! The doctor made some vague reference to "overdoing it," and Peter was on his own again.

For months Peter worried about this experience. Was he going crazy? Was he simply a weak person? Would he have another attack? How soon? What would he do if it happened again? He felt pretty stupid, since the doctor found nothing wrong with him.

These are questions that plague all panic-attack sufferers if they don't get good counsel at the time of their first attack. Very often a panic attack simulates a heart attack: pain in the chest, difficulty in breathing, and a sense of impending death. So the wisest thing to do is go to an emergency room if you are unsure about what is happening to you. Fortunately, these days the outlook is good for panic sufferers. With early identification and aggressive treatment that includes both medication and stress management therapy, sufferers like Peter can look forward to a life relatively free of recurrence.

There is a price to be paid, however. Peter will have to work conscientiously at overcoming his problem, pursue the right form of treatment, and possibly make some drastic lifestyle changes. If he doesn't, chances are that over time he will suffer recurring and worsening panic attacks. Untreated, it could develop into *agoraphobia* (the fear of being in places or situations from which there is no escape).

STRESS AND PANIC

For many years, researchers have pursued an understanding of the connection between stressful life events and the onset of panic attacks. Many studies assessing their relationship have found an abnormally high incidence of stressful life events immediately preceding the first panic attack. One study reported that as many as 91 percent of these attacks had been preceded by high stress. Another found the incidence to be 96 percent.

The main problem with much of this research (even though the findings are conclusive) is that there is still a tendency to think of stress as relating only to the unpleasant or catastrophic events of life. As I have already endeavored to show, and will emphasize throughout this book, the stress that kills is not the stress of crises. These are short-lived and unpleasant enough that we try to avoid them. The stress that does us in is the stress of challenge, high-energy output, and over-commitment. This is as true for panic attacks as it is for heart disease. Exciting stress demands as much adrenaline as fears and threats. And because we enjoy the arousal it brings, we may actually become adrenaline addicts—and move closer to the point of panic.

Prolonged stress, whether pleasant or unpleasant, wears down the system. It exhausts our supply of adrenaline, the most important of the stress hormones, and depletes the natural tranquilizers in our brain that keep us calm and able to go about our business in a controlled manner. When this happens, we become prone to panic—and dependent on *external tranquilizers* for peace of mind.

Perhaps the most famous of all external tranquilizers is Valium. Since it was first introduced, this drug has been a godsend in many ways, a bringer of peace to troubled minds. It has brought problems too, as many who have become dependent on it will attest. Nevertheless, it has often worked miracles in helping people cope with anxiety.

At the time Valium was released on the market, we did not fully understand how or why it worked. It was several years before researchers discovered the reason: Valium calms the brain because it blocks the same receptors blocked by the brain's own natural tranquilizers.

This discovery has revolutionized our understanding of brain medications. It has also pointed us toward the probable cause of panic attacks. Since Valium (and now more potent tranquilizers such as Xanax) block receptors and stop panic attacks, it is very possible that the attacks themselves are brought on by a deficiency of natural tranquilizers.

One way of looking at panic disorders, therefore, is to see them as "deficiency disorders" brought on by too much stress. The deficiency is in natural brain tranquilizers.

This is not the whole story. Some people are highly prone to panic attacks because their brains are either super-sensitive or they have a natural deficiency of tranquilizers. Stress may play a lessor role, but nevertheless an important one, in a small percentage of panic attack sufferers.

MEDICAL CAUSES OF ANXIETY

While modern medicine sometimes overlooks or misdiagnoses anxiety disorders, psychologists often fail to take into account the medical causes of panic. So before you blame stress for all your problems, make sure that the following common physical causes of anxiety problems have been ruled out:

- Hypothyroidism: overactive thyroid gland

- Hypoglycemia: low blood-sugar levels

- Thyrotoxicosis: excessive thyroid hormone in the blood

- Caffeinism: overuse of caffeine (as in coffee, etc.)
- Diabetes Mellitus: disturbed insulin balance
- Depression: serious mood disturbances
- Schizophrenia: serious mental disturbance
- Psychomotor epilepsy: epilepsy affecting one part of the brain
- High blood pressure: elevated pressure in arteries
- Cerebral arteriosclerosis: hardening of the arteries in the brain
- Alcohol withdrawal: all drug withdrawals are anxiety producing
- Cocaine abuse: overuse of cocaine
- Mitral valve prolapse: a common disorder of a heart valve
- Hyperventilation: a disturbance of regular breathing.

This is by no means a complete list of medical conditions that can cause panic attacks, so please consult your physician if you suspect that your problem may have a physical cause. Most of the conditions listed require medical attention of some sort. It stands to reason that if you have a medical problem known to produce an exaggerated anxiety reaction, you should first have this problem attended to. It may very well be the sole cause of your anxiety problem. Even if it isn't, a medical condition may still be contributing indirectly to your anxiety by weakening your tolerance for normal tensions and stress.

An excellent example of how physical factors can bring on anxiety symptoms was reported several years ago in a psychiatric journal. The case concerned a woman (let's call her Evelyn) who loved diet colas, especially those sweetened with a particular artificial sweetener. She drank a half-dozen cans of diet cola each day.

Evelyn took a job as a cook in a restaurant. The kitchen where she worked was unusually hot, so she perspired a lot and boosted her consumption of diet colas to around twenty cans a day.

About a week later, Evelyn began to have anxiety attacks. She felt dizzy and complained of tightness in her chest and had difficulty breathing. She knew enough to realize that her over consumption of diet colas might be the problem, so she immediately cut back to only three or four a day, substituting a non-cola drink. Her symptoms disappeared. To test that this was really the reason for her anxiety, she increased her consumption to twenty colas a day—and her symptoms immediately returned. She was convinced!

Evelyn was wise enough to be alert to possible physical causes for her anxiety. She saved herself a lot of trouble and money in not having to seek treatment. More importantly, she avoided being conditioned by her first few anxiety attacks into becoming an anxiety neurotic.

TREATMENT CONSIDERATIONS

While my purpose in discussing panic anxiety here is not to provide a comprehensive treatment guide but to show its connection to stress, having raised the topic, I feel I should at least point the reader to some treatment guidelines. Obviously, attention to stress matters is important for both prevention and cure of anxiety problems. So in addition to what I will be saying throughout the remainder of this book, the following should also be taken into account.

Help for your anxiety problem begins by diligently looking for the primary cause—whether it is physical, psychological, or behavioral, or all three.

First, remember that achieving a *reduction in the symptoms of panic* may just be the first step toward a final cure, not a cure in itself. Relapses can and will occur and must be accepted as "par for the course." Faithful and persistent adherence to the principles of treatment is absolutely necessary.

Most sufferers fail to find relief because they give up too soon or jump from one treatment to another. Make sure you give each strategy a fair chance before moving on.

Second, it is important to *address the larger stress picture* in your life. You cannot expect to cure your anxiety problem while keeping your stress high. Carry out any suggestions I make in cooperation with whoever is treating you. If you suffer from a panic disorder, you need the objective guidance of a trained professional to coach you to success. The ultimate goal is to bring about a change in lifestyle so that the suggestions I make will become an integral part of your normal life. They should become so natural that you don't even have to think about them. This means, among other things, cooperating with your physician in the use of medication. Panic attacks are so frightening that they easily set up a *fear-of-fear* reaction and it is often necessary to bring them under control as quickly as possible with appropriate medication, including the use of tranquilizers to facilitate healing.

There are several possible dangers in becoming over-dependent on medication, of course. One is that the sufferer may feel so good on the medication that he or she resists addressing the underlying causes of the panic attacks. Lifestyle stress, an abusive environment, or other issues may need to be evaluated, and without the "urgency" of the pain or anxiety, the pressure to change may diminish. Even if you find relief in medication, *don't* neglect these other important issues. If you do, you may find yourself in greater trouble later on when the medication is stopped.

An opposite danger is that a panic sufferer may *resist* taking any prescribed medication. Many well-meaning but strong-willed people who suffer panic attacks refuse to comply with their physician's recommendations. Some are caught up with fears about becoming addicted to the medication. Others see their need for medication as a sign of spiritual failure or weakness and therefore resist taking any medicine.

Listen to me! These beliefs can easily cause you continued suffering and will not help you master your affliction. If a competent professional recommends appropriate medication, and if this medication works to prevent an attack or ultimately cures you of your panic disorder, you owe it to yourself and your loved ones not to sabotage the treatment. While there may be a few who will become dependent on the medication, most do not. If you fear this possibility, then discuss it with your physician!

AVOIDING PANIC ATTACKS

Here are some closing thoughts on how to avoid panic attacks if you find yourself panic-prone or in a stressful situation you cannot avoid:

- *Avoid exercise.* Exercise generally makes you more panic-prone if you are in a panic stage of stress. Otherwise, try a form of exercise that is less aerobic.
- *Avoid caffeine.* Go cold turkey on your caffeine dependency, if necessary, and get over your need for it. It is a strong stimulant, and not what you need.
- *Avoid alcohol.* Alcohol is a depressant that plays havoc with your emotional system. If used as a tranquilizer, it can often become addicting (alcoholism), which simply complicates a panic problem.
- *Avoid smoking.* Nicotine is addictive and aggravates panic attacks.
- *Avoid unnecessary stress.* Make room for plenty of extra sleep and regular relaxation, of the sort I will describe in a later chapter, which will help to increase your natural brain tranquilizers.
- *Avoid any foods or food additives* that seem to make your symptoms worse. By experimenting, find out what food products tend to increase your anxiety—or consult an allergist.
- *Avoid seriousness.* Try to be less intense and take life in stride. Try laughing at yourself, your mistakes, and your circumstances. Humor boosts the brain's natural tranquilizers and releases us from physical and emotional tension. It's hard for the body to maintain a state of anxiety in the face of laughter. I will have more to say about this later.

PART TWO

Diagnosing Your Adrenaline Arousal

"Among all my autopsies (and I have performed well over a thousand), I have never seen a person who died of old age. In fact, *I do not think anyone has died of old age yet.* To permit this would be the ideal accomplishment of medical research. . . .

To die of old age would mean that all the organs of the body had worn out proportionately, merely by having been used too long. This is never the case. We invariably die because one vital part has worn out too early in proportion to the rest of the body. . . .

The lesson seems to be that, as far as man can regulate his life by voluntary actions, he should seek to equalize stress throughout his being!

The human body—like the tires on a car or the rug on a floor—wears longest when it wears evenly."

—HANS SELYE
The Stress of Life

The Symptoms of Distress

There is no such thing as stress only in the mind. Stress begins in the mind but ends in the body. This is important to remember. In this chapter, I want to look at some of the specific physical effects of stress so that you will be able to evaluate the seriousness of your stress problem.

THE BODY'S DEFENSE SYSTEM

The human body is designed with an important system to protect us from stress. All living organisms have such a system, which reaches its highest state of efficiency and intricacy in humans. There are three components to this protective system:

1. An *alarm system* designed to sound a warning when something goes wrong. Pain plays a role in this system's operation, signaling when body tissue is being damaged.

2. An *activating system* to prepare for action in response to the alarm. This is an emergency system triggered and sustained by adrenaline arousal. It prepares us for the "fight or flight" response.

3. A *recovery system* designed to provide healing, recuperation, and revitalization. Neglect of this recovery system leads to premature heart disease and many other painful consequences of stress.

To understand how these systems operate, let's look at a typical stress reaction in a patient I will call Janice. Janice is thirty-two years old. Like so many women today, she is trying to combine a career with parenting. She is married to a businessman, has two sons ages eight and six, and is enrolled in graduate school in pursuit of a degree in social work.

It is Monday morning and Janice is trying to get the family off to work and school so she can get to her class. She gets up at six in the morning while her husband, Jim, is still snoozing in bed. While he is sometimes helpful with the boys, Jim just doesn't have a mother's touch when it comes to preparing school lunches, preparing breakfasts to feed two little mouths, or putting pants on two little bodies the right way.

This particular morning is a bad one. Janice worked on a class paper until late the night before and didn't get enough sleep, so she is tired. The boys are noisier than usual and also slower in dressing themselves. Janice loses her patience, gets angry, and yells at them. They pay no attention, so she yells louder.

"You're going to make me late this morning!" she yells for the third time. Jim appears on the scene, still dressed in his pajamas and wiping sleep from his eyes. He tries to help by saying, "Come on, Janice, they're only little boys! It doesn't matter if they are late for school."

"It does matter to me!" Janice screams back. And then it hits. A sharp, stabbing pain in the back of the neck, a tight band around the head. She can feel a classic tension headache coming on. She's had it on many Monday mornings before. And she knows it's going to be a painful day.

The pain is signaling that Janice's *alarm system* has kicked in. It's telling her that she is under too much stress. Just like a bell clanging to warn of a fire, the alarm system serves a very important function—if you pay attention to it. Unfortunately, most of us don't. We reach for the painkiller to silence the bell . . . and don't attend to the fire.

Janice goes to the bathroom. *I'd better take some aspirin right now before this headache gets any worse,* she thinks.

She goes back to the kitchen. The boys still aren't ready to go. "Now that's it! I've had enough! If you boys don't hurry, I'm going to punish you."

She moves into high gear. In a few quick moves she has everything organized. Before the boys know it, they've been bundled into the car and are on their way to school.

This is Janice's *activating system* in action. Her stress has made her more efficient, energized, and action-oriented. Her adrenaline is pumping stronger than ever. She can move quickly, make snap decisions, and even temporarily suppress her headache. The high level of activity feels good to her. The adrenaline almost gives her a "high." More importantly, she feels in control again.

Janice drops the boys off at school, races to the university, and gets to class just as the professor is about to begin his lecture. She settles into her chair. Slowly her adrenaline level drops. She yawns. No more action is needed, just a quiet receiving of knowledge. But now the headache starts to come back, only more intensely. She feels a flutter in her chest, as if her heart had skipped a beat. Suddenly she feels tired and old—all worn out and listless. She yawns again. *I wish I could just go back to bed and sleep the rest of the day,* she thinks.

She is now under the control of her *recovery system.* Her adrenaline has continued to drop and her body is demanding time for recuperation. She is in desperate need of rest. Unfortunately, before bedtime there will be many more occasions for her alarm, activation, and recovery systems to be triggered and go through their cycle. It's going to be a tough day for Janice.

COOPERATE WITH YOUR BODY

These three reactions—*alarm, activation,* and *recovery*—are "automatic." They happen without our having to think about them, and this is why they can cause us so much trouble. They do their thing without our knowing or thinking about them, so we don't always realize how important it is to cooperate with them.

To understand how the protection system functions, fix in your mind the following sequence of reactions to stress:

1. Alarm

2. Activation

3. Recovery

So that we can learn to be more aware of where we are at any time, let's examine each system separately:

1. *Alarm.* The purpose of the alarm system is to warn us when our bodies are being pushed beyond their normal limits. The body is provided with many "pain" signals, a form of discomfort that is designed to warn us. Unfortunately, in our performance-oriented culture we've come to believe that pain is an "enemy" rather than a "friend." When we experience pain, we try to remove it rather than welcome it and heed its warning. Seldom do we stop and say, " The pain is telling me to slow down; let me pay attention to its message before I take a painkiller to get rid of it."

   Janice's headache was a sign that her alarm system was going off loud and clear. She should have slowed down, realized she was under too much pressure, reordered her priorities, asked her husband for help, and "quieted" her hurried heart. This would have made for a more peaceful atmosphere and would have helped her avoid a painful stress experience.

2. *Activation.* Sometimes, but not always, it is important to allow yourself to move to the activation stage. Activation occurs when adrenaline is recruited and the "fight or flight" reaction triggered. We are mobilized to act. We become physically stronger (which can be dangerous if we are angry) and mentally sharper. Notice I said "sharper," not "more creative or innovative." When adrenaline is high we are enabled to be more focused and directed. Snap decisions are easy. Thoughtful decisions are impossible. In the emergency mode, speed is what is required. However, mistakes also come easily.

   Activation is appropriate when the situation warrants it. Emergencies and other pressing demands require that we act. But we are not designed to stay activated all the time. Sooner or later, and the sooner the better, we must move to the next system.

3. *Recovery.* This the most misunderstood and neglected part of the system. We don't cooperate very well with recovery

because we have been taught to feel guilty whenever we indulge it. Also, the lowering level of adrenaline during recovery is invariably accompanied by a feeling of depression. And we just don't like feeling depressed—even when the feeling is a natural part of a healthy stress response. It is also during the recovery stage that many of the more painful consequences of stress are felt. While our adrenaline is up, we are protected from pain. When it drops we are not, and we begin to suffer from the negative effects of stress, such as headaches or diarrhea.

The depression accompanying the recovery state is commonly called the "post-adrenaline blues," and it is not unlike the anticlimax we experience after we've had a "mountaintop" experience. Have you ever had a very exhilarating experience? If you have, you will recall the feeling of letdown that followed it. The drop of your adrenaline signals a mild depression that aids in disengaging you and forcing you to rest. It is really your friend! Knowing how to cooperate with the recovery stage is the focus of Part Three of this book, so I won't pursue it any further here—except to say that when the post-adrenaline slump comes, the sooner you allow yourself to "let down" the quicker your recovery will be. The more you fight it, the longer it will last.

IF YOU DON'T COOPERATE . . .

What if you do not heed the alarm system, limit the workings of the activating system, and cooperate with the recovery system? There is only one answer: You develop stress disease. This is the penalty for ignoring the balance that this system is trying to enforce.

Where will the disease take its toll? The body is like a chain of many links. Even though it has been very carefully made, there is almost always one link that is weaker than the others. When subjected to strain, the body—like a chain—will snap at its weakest point. In the same way, each of us, because of our unique set of genes and the ways we've learned to react to stress, will show our stress response in a unique way. For one person it may be headaches, for another ulcers.

Before I explore some of the unique ways we each suffer from stress, I suggest that you take a moment to write down some notes about your own unique way of experiencing stress. You will find the next section more beneficial if you do this. Ask yourself: What is the *first* symptom I feel when I am stressed?

How does this symptom start? *When* does it begin? Does it *move* from one part of my body to another? *How long* does it last? See if you can recognize the sequence of alarm, activation, and recovery.

THE SYMPTOMS OF DISTRESS

In chapters 1 and 2, we examined how stress generally affects the body. Now we will look more specifically at the variety of symptoms that accompany stress disease.

Let me caution you to be very careful at this point. While it is my intention to increase your awareness of stress disease and help you recognize stress symptoms, it is very easy to misread verbal descriptions and either exaggerate the severity of minor symptoms or minimize the importance of major ones. Consult a physician or psychologist if you are at all concerned about any of these symptoms.

Figure 3 summarizes the effects of stress on various parts of the body. Examine the figure so as to understand the change occurring in each organ, then read the following list of symptoms associated with these organs.

1. *Brain:* generalized panic and anxiety, migraine headaches

2. *Heart:* rapid heartbeat, skipped beats, raised blood pressure, thumping and mild mid-sternum pain, dizziness and light headedness from high blood pressure, palpitations

3. *Stomach and Intestines:* general gastric distress, feelings of nausea, acid stomach and heartburn, diarrhea (chronic and acute), some forms of colitis, indigestion, constipation, churning

4. *Muscles:* neck ache and shoulder pain, headaches, stiff neck, teeth grinding, jaw joint pain (transmandibular joint

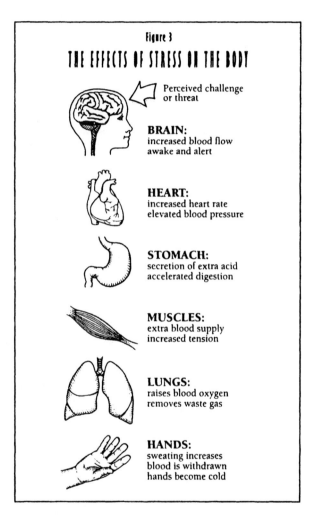

Figure 3

THE EFFECTS OF STRESS ON THE BODY

Perceived challenge
or threat

BRAIN:
increased blood flow
awake and alert

HEART:
increased heart rate
elevated blood pressure

STOMACH:
secretion of extra acid
accelerated digestion

MUSCLES:
extra blood supply
increased tension

LUNGS:
raises blood oxygen
removes waste gas

HANDS:
sweating increases
blood is withdrawn
hands become cold

syndrome), high and low back pain, generalized pain in arms
and legs

5. *Hands and Skin:* cold extremities, increased sweating, skin
   eruptions

6. *Lungs/Respiratory Problems:* some asthma, hyperventilation
   syndrome, shortness of breath

7. *General:* feelings of "trembling," fear of impending doom,
   inability to sit for very long, squirming and fidgeting,

foot-tapping, pacing, feelings of fatigue, lack of energy or heaviness, heightened irritability and anger, racing thoughts, daydreaming, indecisiveness, sleep disruption.

Which are the more common symptoms of overstress? An interesting study by Drs. Jonathan C. Smith and Jeffrey M. Seidel of Roosevelt University examined the symptoms reported by more than twelve hundred subjects and broke them down to find the more common ones.

Smith and Seidel found eighteen common symptom clusters. The most notable was *gastric distress*, followed by *disturbed cardio-respiratory activity, restless activity, self-conscious activity, feelings of fatigue and lack of energy,* and *headaches.* Other factors included *backache; skin difficulties; shoulder, neck, and back tensions;* and *trembling and shaking.* Of all these factors, gastric distress was the greatest, being four times more common than the next highest. This complaint included *stomach discomfort, pain, excess secretion of acid,* and *churning.* There was no difference in frequency of occurrence between males and females.

This is a formidable list of symptoms, and since many of them can also be caused by problems other than stress, it usually takes a trained professional to make an accurate differential diagnosis. It's a good idea to seek professional help if you are worried about these symptoms.

It is possible, however, to use the above list to gain a general picture of your level of stress.

Figure 4 presents an objective test to help you do this. The instructions are simple: Think back over the past several months, then read through the list of symptoms, asking yourself whether any of them have been a bother to you. Rate the intensity of each symptom according to the scale and write the appropriate number under "Rating." When you have finished, add up your "score" and compare it to the chart in Appendix 1. The total score will be somewhere between zero and sixty. The higher the score, the greater your level of distress.

Obviously, a test like this is subject to distortion by either exaggeration or under-valuation of a symptom. If you don't trust your judgment about yourself, then ask a trusted friend to go

Figure 4
STMPTOMS OF DISTRESS

Answer the questions listed below according to the following scale

Score   **Description**

0   I do not experience this symptom at all
1   I sometimes (perhaps once a month) experience this symptom
2   I experience this symptom more than once a month, but not more than once a week
3   I experience this symptom often (more than once a week)

Symptom   **Score**

1   Do you experience headaches of any sort? _____

2   Do you experience tension or stiffness in your neck, shoulders, jaws, arms, hands, legs, or stomach? _____

3   Do you have nervous tics, or do you tremble? _____

4   Do you feel sour heart, thumping, or racing? _____

5   Do you get irregular heartbeats or does your heart skip beats? _____

6   Do you have difficulty breathing at times? _____

7   Do you ever get dizzy or light-headed? _____

8   Do you feel like you have a lump in your throat or you have to clear it? _____

9   Do you get colds, the flu, or hoarseness? _____

10   Are you bothered by indigestion, nausea, or discomfort in sour stomach? _____

11   Do you have diarrhea or constipation? _____

12   Do you bite your nails? _____

13   Do you have difficulty falling or staying asleep? _____

14   Do you wake up feeling tired? _____

15   Are your hands or feet cold? _____

16   Do you grind or grit your teeth or do your jaws ache? _____

17   Are you prone to excessive sweating? _____

18   Are you angry or irritable? _____

19   Do you feel a lot of general pain (back pain, stomach pain, head pain, muscle pain, etc.)? _____

20   Have you become aware of increased anxiety, worry, fidgeting, or restlessness? _____

Total Score _____

over the test with you. In dialogue with this friend, you might just be more accurate and honest.

Remember that even though your score may not be very high, you might still be heading for one of the "hidden" forms of stress disease. As I have pointed out, the excitement of high adrenaline arousal can mask the insidious damage going on in the heart, vascular system, or stomach. High adrenaline often masks pain, and habitually stressed people may not always be aware of the symptoms of distress until stress disease is far advanced.

TYPES OF HEADACHES

Since headaches are such a common consequence of overstress, they deserve special discussion here.

There are many types of headaches (at least fifteen categories are recognized), but not all of them are stress-related. The most common form of headache is known by various terms—*tension headache, muscle contraction headache,* or *stress headache.* These all mean the same thing, and in each case *stress* is the cause.

Such headaches afflict between fifty and a hundred million people in the United States. At some time or another everyone suffers from periods of tension headache. If you haven't yet, be patient! Your time is coming!

Because *migraine headaches* are also quite common, let me point out that there are important differences between *migraines* and *tension headaches.* The two are often confused with each other because those who actually have tension headaches prefer to call them "migraines." There is less stigma, I suppose, attached to the label "migraines." You don't feel quite so responsible for them!

The picture is further complicated by the fact that both migraines and tension headaches can be *triggered* by stress.

Obviously a test like this is subject to distortion by either over-exaggerating your symptoms or under-valuing them. If you don't trust your judgment, then ask a close and trusted friend to go over the test with you. In dialogue with this friend, you might just be more accurate.

Remember that even though your score may not be very high, you might still be heading for one of the "hidden" forms of stress disease! Very often the excitement of high adrenaline arousal can mask the insidious damage going on in the heart, vascular system, or stomach. High adrenaline can also mask pain. Highly aroused people can sometimes avoid all the symptoms of stress until the disease is very far advanced.

HEADACHES AND DISTRESS

Migraines are typically felt in one side of the head and often include feelings of nausea or vomiting. The pain is sharp and throbbing. Migraines can come on at any time, even waking the sufferer in the middle of the night.

Tension headaches, on the other hand, are dull and "pressured." They can eventually cover the whole head, though many feel them starting over the eyes or at the back of the head where there are muscles that become tense during stress. They often come on toward the end of the day and sleep helps to relieve them, unlike migraines. Often the pain feels like a tight band or a squeezing around the head, because it is really the muscles of the face and head that are causing the pain.

Sometimes the pain comes from the joints in the jaw and the muscles in the temple area. The inability to open the mouth wide enough to accept three fingers vertically is taken as a sign of reduced jaw-joint mobility due to stress, but be careful when you do this test if you have big fingers! Another sign of jaw trouble can be detected as a popping or cracking sound as the mouth is opened and closed. Since a tightening of the jaw muscles is often related to stress, professional help should be sought as soon as possible. In the long run, it can literally wear away your jaw joints.

Tension headaches can be caused by stress in a number of ways. First, the sustained higher muscle tension produced by adrenaline and neural triggering can create pain when the muscle fibers become fatigued. Second, the heightened tension releases pain-producing chemicals into the muscle fibers. Third, the blood supply can be reduced to these muscles, presumably because the blood is needed by these muscles for "fight or flight."

Migraine headaches (and there are several varieties) are caused by inflammation and contraction of blood vessels in the head and brain. The predisposition to migraines is mostly inherited, but stress can trigger migraine headaches in susceptible persons.

Just before or during a migraine attack, the hands often get cold. Migraine sufferers also tend to have chronic cold hands and feet. Knowledge of this fact can help in distinguishing migraines from tension headaches.

Cluster headaches (a variation of migraine) are much less common than tension or classic migraine headaches. They are called "clusters" because they come in groups, occurring once or several times a day for a few days, then going away. The pain is very severe, and men suffer from these cluster headaches five times more often than women. Whether or not cluster headaches can be triggered or aggravated by stress is not clear, although I suspect they are much less stress-related than either tension or migraine headaches.

Diseases of the eyes, ears, nose, or bones of the skull and neck can cause head pain, as can infections and tumors. A physician can readily diagnose these. Obviously, they are not stress-related.

Headaches more difficult to diagnose can come from environmental conditions or foods. Stress may or may not play a role in these instances.

Foods that cause headaches in some people include egg whites, caffeine, ice cream, sugar, and hot dogs. Just how these foods trigger headaches and whether stress aggravates them is not known. Presumably, there is some allergic or other reaction that is very specific to the affected person. I know, for instance, that strong fluorescent lights such as those found in supermarkets, trigger headaches in me. When I am under stress, the headaches seem worse. The same is true for those who work for prolonged periods under such lights. I suspect that I have some marked sensitivity to the rapid flashing produced by these lights in contrast to incandescent lights, and that this becomes a "stressor" to my body.

ALLERGIES AND STRESS

Allergies in general can produce headaches, as well as myriad other reactions such as hay fever, asthma, gastrointestinal disturbance, hives, and behavior problems. An allergic substance is anything that alters the reaction of tissues in some people while being innocuous to others. If everyone suffered the same reaction, it would be called a "poison." Because it affects only some people, it is called an allergen. For the sufferer, it is a poison nevertheless.

I am very allergic to the fine fur on the skin of peaches. If I touch a peach, I break out in an itching rash that nothing can soothe. The effect is immediate. Other types of allergens have a delayed effect.

To what extent is an allergic reaction or allergic headache stress-related? We have no proof at this point, but there is abundant anecdotal evidence that when someone is highly stressed, *any allergic predisposition* may be greatly aggravated. So while stress may not be the cause of allergies, it could certainly be a trigger. So, if you suffer from allergies you should pay special attention to the stress in your life!

EFFECTS OF CHRONIC STRESS

There are three more generalized effects of stress I would like to mention, because they can account for so many of the ailments we suffer today. An understanding of them can be very helpful in recognizing stress.

When stress is chronic—that is, when it is continuous and doesn't let up or allow the body adequate time for recovery—the following happens:

1. *The immune system becomes depleted.* The immune system is that part of the body designed to fight off disease and infection. Certain hormones, white blood cells, and a host of other complex mechanisms are designed to fight off all intruders in body tissue. There are even a few hormones that help facilitate how the body combats disease under the special conditions of stress. Now, when the total body is under duress, as it is when stress is chronic, something must be sacrificed in order to protect the body as a whole. The immune system then becomes depleted.

What is the consequence of this? Under prolonged stress, we tend to become sick more frequently. Infection takes over, the flu strikes when we don't expect it, and the body does not heal as rapidly as in times of less stress.

There is even strong evidence to suggest that certain cancers grow more rapidly in stressed-out people. And it is suspected that other disorders, such as rheumatoid arthritis—are caused—or at least aggravated, by stress. Separation from a loved one, marital difficulties, or general emotional strain all seem to be aggravating factors in much disease because these conditions put us under stress.

How can we restore a healthy immune system? As we will see, the answer lies in learning to manage stress so that it is more constructive in our lives. One very important rejuvenator of the immune system is worthy of comment here because it is so little known. Recent research has found an important link between sleep and the immune system. It appears that during sleep, a chemical called *macrophages,* which is known to activate cells, is produced. These macrophages rush to the sites of infection where they remove bacteria and foreign bodies from the blood and damaged tissues. Macrophages in turn make *interleukin*—a chemical that regulates fever and signals other disease-fighting cells called lymphocytes that are needed at the sites of bacterial invasion.

So what has this got to do with stress? Well, high stress interferes with sleep—thus interfering with the body's healing. If you want a healthy body, then deal with your stress and make sure you get a good night's sleep. I'll have a lot more to say about this later!

2. *The anti-pain system becomes depleted.* This is another unexpected (but not unexplainable) reaction to prolonged stress. In recent years, it has been discovered that the brain has its own analgesics circulating within. These pain-killing hormones, called *endorphins* (short for *endogenous morphine*), are as powerful as morphine. They help us control our pain. Without them, we would be constantly racked by excruciating agony.

During some types of stress, especially the short-lived acute forms, the body may initially produce more endorphins, thus helping us cope with our pain. Elevated adrenaline, however, can block pain in another way.

For instance, if you experienced a sudden emergency, you would find you had remarkable strength and pain control. Let's imagine you are camping in the mountains with a friend. While you are out hiking one day, your friend falls and is seriously injured. The only way to get help is to run three or four miles to the nearest ranger station. It's bitterly cold and you feel exhausted, yet you will find you are able to run the distance very fast and feel no pain at all from the thorns you tramp on or the toes you stub. This is because your body "ignores" pain during times of heightened arousal. It focuses on the immediate crisis and your brain blocks out all other signals. Your adrenaline is working its fantastic magic in times of high stress.

But the same pain-killing reaction is not true for chronic stress. When the crisis is unrelenting, the endorphins become depleted. *Awareness of pain increases, and tolerance for discomfort decreases.* This is one of the reasons why stress-related illnesses are so often linked to feelings of pain all over the body.

3. *The anti-anxiety system becomes depleted.* Just as the brain has endorphins to inhibit pain, it also has its own tranquilizers to inhibit anxiety. Under prolonged stress, however, these natural tranquilizers become depleted, and anxiety feelings go up. As explained in chapter 4, this can cause panic attacks. The mind becomes increasingly obsessed with petty problems and troubling thoughts keep going round and round like a stuck record.

MEDICATION ISN'T THE ANSWER

These three adverse effects of chronic stress—*reduced immune defense, increased pain,* and *increased anxiety*—are as common as grass in our stressed-out culture. And while a variety of chemical weapons (medication) can help protect us from their damaging effects—including antibiotics to replace the depleted immune system, analgesics to kill pain, and tranquilizers to take away anxiety—if we do not deal adequately with the source of the problem, namely stress, we only aid in our self-destruction.

These three major types of medication, together with antacids to dilute stomach acids, are the most commonly consumed medicines today. Vast quantities are prescribed by almost every physician in practice. Unfortunately, they all give testimony to the fact that we are a stress-riddled society.

Actually, the physical consequences of stress can have a positive effect if we learn to see them as warning signals and heed their messages. If you think about it, they are all designed to protect us. The increased proneness to illness, the extra pain, and the restless anxiety should all cause us to pull back and disengage from our stress. They are telling us we are overdoing things and may even help to direct us to find a solution.

Since realizing that my body is intelligently designed, I have changed my attitude to pain and try to listen to the discomfort my body creates when I am under too much stress. Rather than rushing out to buy more painkiller, I attend to the pressures in my life. I force myself to slow down, change my priorities, and relinquish responsibilities that are not mine alone. Above all, I try to maintain a positive attitude—and a positive attitude, especially when coupled with a strong personal faith, is good for every ailment we frail humans fall heir to. It gives life purpose and meaning and minimizes the feeling of helplessness. Helplessness, as we have yet to see, is the greatest source of stress we humans can experience!

Are You an Adrenaline Addict?

Every day around four in the afternoon, Terrence begins to feel restless. He gets edgy, fidgets at the lathe which is his work tool, and begins watching the clock. That last hour of the day passes as slowly as eternity. It's time for his "fix," and he can't wait for the clock to strike five so he can head for the track.

What is his problem? Terrence is hooked on running. He runs at least five miles a day, sometimes ten. And when too much time elapses between his last run and the next, he gets "antsy."

"I knew I was a running junkie when I realized I structured my whole life around my time at the track. I do it for the 'high' it gives me. There is something exhilarating about running. And it's better than spending my life in a bar drinking," Terrence says proudly.

Like many others, Terrence has a "hidden" addiction. He's hooked on his own adrenaline!

THE ADDICTIVE URGE

Terrence is not alone in his dependency. Literally thousands of us are hooked on some activity or interest that we feel compelled to indulge in. Just as an alcoholic is addicted to alcohol or the workaholic to work, the adrenaline addict depends on some activity for the "kick" it gives him. It may just be a psychological dependence or it may be a full blown physiological addiction, but it is as real as any addiction. Whatever the underlying mechanism, the result is always the same: we don't feel normal unless we're doing our "special" activity!

A friend of mine, for instance, is hooked on mountain climbing. Ever since he can remember he has craved being on the peak of some mountain or other. "When I get to the top I feel ecstatic," he will tell you euphorically.

One client of mine is a "chocoholic," and another is hooked on collecting bottle tops. There was a time when I thought my wife was hooked on crocheting. Every free moment she had was given to the nimble fingering of a plastic stick with a hook on the end that goes in and out of deftly formed loops. "Why do you do it?" I asked her once. "Because I enjoy it," she profoundly replied. Who can argue with that?

While many of these activities are simply psychological outlets for tension or anxiety and may even be healthy, some seem to meet a deeper need because they produce a high level of pleasure that is a form of escape. When this happens, you have a *true* addiction, not just a pleasurable habit. Whenever pleasure is used to create a feeling that fosters escape, it is more than innocent. You know it is an addiction when you suffer withdrawal symptoms when deprived of the activity.

But can we really compare, say, a craving for chocolate or a runner's "high" with alcoholism or drug addiction? Of course, there are obvious and important differences. For one thing, we need to define our terms before we talk about addictions. Different terminologies are used to denote different kinds of habits or addictions. So here are the more important terms and what they mean:

- *Dependency* usually refers only to a psychological need for something, although who knows what complex body chemistry underlies all our pleasure cravings!

- *An addiction* technically refers to a physical need for something—such as a chemical addiction that can produce extreme physical discomfort when the body is deprived of the substance.

- *A habit* is merely something we like to do over and over again. Habits usually give us pleasure, but not always.
- *A craving* is a very strong desire for something. The term usually applies to something like food or drink, but it can also apply to bungie-cord jumping or shopping!

In many ways these all overlap because underlying each of them is the human need for pleasure and a tendency to get "hooked" on anything that gives us intense pleasure—whether the pleasure is psychological (the satisfaction of knowing that you didn't kill yourself, jumping off a high bridge while attached to just a slender elastic umbilical cord) or physiological (the delight of a gourmet meal). Many experts now agree that almost all pleasurable activity can become "addicting" (as both dependency and addiction), because the mechanisms of addiction are centered in the pleasure center of the brain. This fantastic center through which information about everything pleasurable passes, whether it be cocaine, caffeine, or common habits, is the center that makes us crave more and more of both good and bad things.

Eating, sleeping, walking, riding, sex, hobbies, TV-watching, smoking, video games, gossip—all have the ability to hook us simply because they are activities that give us pleasure. Even fishing, which produces in some a profound state of relaxation, can be habit-forming. Both *stimulating* and *tranquilizing* activities can create a dependency that can lead to an addiction, even though they produce opposite effects. What they have in common is *pleasure.*

Is this necessarily bad? No, obviously not—at least not always. Most of the activities I have listed are essentially harmless. And some—such as exercise and sleep—are in themselves beneficial. Who could complain about being addicted to sleep? And Terrence is probably right in his assessment that running is better for him than spending the equivalent amount of time in a bar.

But the trouble with any kind of dependent or addictive behavior is that people can come to use it for other purposes, such as an escape from problems and to relieve anxiety. This causes them to rely on the dependent activity too heavily and to "run away" from their problems and the reality of their lives. It is this aspect of addiction that is unhealthy—as well as the physical damage that it might do.

Also, people who become addicted to experiences suffer from "withdrawal" if they can't get their "fix." We don't understand the complex body chemistry underlying this. We just know that it happens.

Research being done at a number of universities is beginning to show that the mechanisms underlying a dependency on activities, not just drugs, may actually be very similar to those involving drugs and alcohol addiction or cigarette smoking.

"There are biological, psychological, and sociological common denominators between drug abuse and other habitual behaviors," writes psychologist Dr. Harvey Milkman of the Metropolitan State College in Denver. "You are addicted if you cannot control when you start or stop an activity." In this respect, *all addictions are alike*—they rob us of control over our lives.

ADDICTED TO ADRENALINE?

This now brings me to the central question raised in this chapter. I believe that dependency on certain "exciting" activities, be they hobbies, games, or challenges, has one feature in common with the well-known addictions such as alcoholism or drug abuse. *They are also drug addictions*—only the drug is from within, not without the body.

What I mean is that it is actually possible for us to become *addicted to our own adrenaline!* We can get hooked on the pleasurable "high" that comes from the workings of the body's own defense system. Both psychological dependence on the excitement of adrenaline arousal, as well as physical addiction to the hormone, can be involved. And this addiction can powerfully control our actions and emotions.

The addiction starts when the body produces large amounts of adrenaline and related hormones under conditions of stress. As we have seen in previous chapters, this adrenaline creates a surge of energy to help the body respond to the stressful challenge. And as we have also seen, this surge of activity often feels good! Pain is suppressed and we feel exhilarated and powerful.

Because the adrenaline response can be intensely pleasurable, however, and human beings have a tendency to become dependent on anything pleasurable, it is possible for us to actually become hooked on the "adrenaline high" to the point that we crave it more and more. We learn to "psych" ourselves up to a high level of excitement just to feel good. And the danger is that we become dependent on the body's emergency system to carry out our normal, everyday activities. When deprived of the adrenaline high, we suffer from "withdrawal"—usually a "post-adrenaline depression."

Obviously, the chemicals of the body that cause the addiction to adrenaline are many and complex, and there are undoubtedly psychological as well as physiological factors at work. My purpose here is not to give a lesson in either biochemistry or psychology. But I believe there is no other way to account for why we become as dependent on certain activities as on alcohol, cocaine, or nicotine. I know that exciting projects affect me as powerfully as drugs do others! It is logical to assume that the body's "pleasure center" (an actual location in the brain through which pleasure signals are sent) is being stimulated by its own internal chemistry.

The idea of "adrenaline addiction" has important implications for how we deal with stress. The very same adrenaline that gives us "kicks" is also the drug that causes us distress when used to excess. And we all have the potential to become hooked on it. If we do not learn to "back off" from our adrenaline "highs," the very pleasure we derive from even basically healthy endeavors can be a slow form of self destruction.

I am often asked about the so-called "adrenaline rush," so allow me to make a few comments on how this is related to stress. The adrenaline rush is actually the release of two hormones: *adrenaline* (80 percent) and *noradrenaline* (20 percent). They act to directly stimulate various organs. Their function is to "rev" the body and make it more effective in coping with a challenge—like racing or fighting. Intense exercise also causes such a "rush."

Is there any value in such a surge of energy? Only in emergencies—like when being mugged or running from a fire! If prolonged, it does the same as all abuse of the adrenal system: It wears down the body faster!

Many upstanding people would be shocked to discover they were "addicted" to anything, let alone their own adrenaline.

They abhor the idea that some medication or artificial stimulant would have them bound in its clutches. Yet they are oblivious to a dangerous addiction that can develop without their even being aware of it!

How can you tell if you are addicted to adrenaline? A reliable indicator is having one or more of the following reactions concerning a specific activity:

- You would rather engage in your activity than sleep.
- When you stop your activity, you feel restless.
- You only feel excited or encouraged when you engage in your activity; at other times you feel "low."
- Your activity helps you forget your problems.
- Whenever you feel depressed, you turn to your activity to make you feel better.
- You fantasize a lot about your activity when you are away from it.

The more times you answer "Yes" to the above questions, the greater the likelihood that you are "hooked" on the adrenaline high that activity gives you.

WORKAHOLISM AS ADRENALINE ADDICTION

It is especially easy for many of us to get hooked on the challenges of an exciting job or career, because attachment to work is so highly valued in our work-centered culture. While "workaholism" can sometimes be an escape from home problems or basic insecurities, most often it is nothing more than an addiction to the adrenaline rushes brought on by challenge and competition.

Competition is as much a part of the American way of life as apple pie and baseball. Schools and businesses depend on and utilize the "high" that a challenge can create. They know how to open the floodgates and cause vast quantities of adrenaline to be released into the bloodstream by capitalizing on the feeling of exhilaration that adrenaline can bring.

But there is a black lining to this euphoric cloud. What we are doing, says Stanley Sunderwirth, a prominent biochemist, is "drugging ourselves" into an artificial form of existence. "The addicting activity produces changes in the brain that are the same as or similar to changes produced by drugs. The effect is pleasure—an artificial high gear."[1] The adrenaline activity that we depend on to help us work long hours and "go the extra mile" to achieve some nebulous feeling of success produces chemical changes in the brain (and possibly other parts of the body also) that are similar to the changes produced by drugs. The short-term effect is pleasure, but the long-term effect may well be stress disease!

WITHDRAWAL SYMPTOMS OF ADRENALINE ADDICTION

Just like any drug addiction, adrenaline addiction can cause withdrawal symptoms whenever the body is deprived of a state of high adrenaline.

I will never forget the first time my wife and I went to Hawaii. I was to teach a two-week course to a group of ministers as part of our Doctor of Ministry program. We had decided to take an extra week and have a short vacation before I began to teach, because I had just been through a very demanding schedule.

My wife reports that for the first three days of our vacation, I was extremely restless when we were not out sightseeing. Not having anything "to do," I paced around the hotel room a lot. I sat down for a while, got up, walked to the window, stared at the ocean. I switched on the TV, picked up a book, put it down, and said I was going for a walk. I walked down the seven flights of stairs, looked in a few shop windows, then took the elevator back to the room.

I was restless and fidgety. In short, I was experiencing adrenaline withdrawal. My mind and body craved excitement—or at least something entertaining.

Fortunately, I understood the nature of my restlessness, so I did my best to cooperate with what my body was doing—I went "cold turkey" and allowed the withdrawal process to reset my body to a state of lower arousal.

And it worked! By the fourth day I began to calm down. I felt more relaxed and at peace than I had for a long time. My sleeping got better and I became more patient. By the end of the week, I was a normal person again. My wife vouches for this!

It is not uncommon for people to suffer from such withdrawal symptoms during the early part of a vacation. What does this say? I think it says that a lot of us are adrenaline addicts to some extent. This is especially true of those who are Type A, because we produce more adrenaline in the first place.

The symptoms of adrenaline withdrawal are easy to recognize. These include:

- a *strong compulsion* to be "doing something" while at home or on vacation
- an *obsession with thoughts* about what remains undone
- a *feeling of vague guilt* while resting
- *fidgeting, restlessness, pacing, leg kicking* or *fast gum chewing*, an *inability to concentrate* for very long on any relaxing activity, *feelings of irritability and aggravation*
- a *vague (or sometimes profound) feeling of depression* whenever you stop an activity.

ADRENALINE FATIGUE

One of the purposes of the stress response is to say to the body, "Prepare for lots of action; get the fuel level up; we've got a battle to fight." The stress hormones are powerful mediators in the conversion of stored sugar into energy. Stored sugar, known as "glycogen," has to be converted to glucose before the body can use it. In response to a demand, the body uses its marvelous intelligence to decide how much glucose is needed. Adrenaline and the other stress hormones then act as the stimulating signals for the conversion.

Adrenaline also contracts the muscular layer in the walls of the arteries. This, together with speeded-up heart rate, raises the blood pressure and stimulates increased respiration. The extra oxygen, carried in the blood, is needed for increased muscle activity.

Normally, *what goes up must come down.* As we saw in the previous chapter, the level of adrenaline drops as the demand for it passes. At this time we normally experience the symptoms of discomfort or distress that come with the wear-and-tear of stress. While adrenaline is elevated, the body seems to be able to fight off disease and discomfort. But when it drops, the body returns all systems to a normal level of arousal. It is at this point that headaches, diarrhea, fatigue, illness, rapid heartbeats, skipped beats, depression, and generalized anxiety are felt. And again, this is part of the normal process of recovery from stress.

However, when the adrenaline level remains high for an extended period of time, a state of "hypoadrenia"—adrenaline fatigue—can set in. The prolonged state of stress causes the adrenal cortex or outer layer of the adrenal gland to become enlarged, important lymph nodes to shrink, and the stomach and intestines to become irritated. The adrenal system eventually "crashes" and forces the victim into a state of prolonged and severe fatigue.

Thomas is typical of someone suffering from adrenaline exhaustion or fatigue. A mechanical engineer who works for a large manufacturing company, he was placed in charge of a new factory and told, "We are way behind in our production schedule: You must do everything possible to get us back on target."

At first, Thomas loved the challenge; it brought out the best in him. He saw problems as challenges to be fought and conflicts as tournaments to be won. He started to work longer hours because he couldn't accomplish everything in a normal day. He would often spend whole nights on the job, creating a makeshift bedroom in his office. His wife complained a little, but Thomas seemed so happy in his work that she felt guilty for wanting him to come home every night, especially since the factory was a long drive from their home. No matter how hard Thomas worked and whatever progress he made, his superiors demanded more. If he achieved a 5 percent increase in productivity one week, his supervisor at head office asked for 10 percent the next.

Then one day everything crashed for Thomas. Walking back to his office late in the afternoon, he began to panic. An intense feeling of fear and impending doom overtook him; he began to tremble and could not stand up. So he sat down on a low wall, thinking, *What is happening to me?* He felt a great wave of tired-ness wash over him, as if he were drowning and had no fight left in him. He even thought, *How marvelous it would be to lie down and stop living!*

A colleague found Thomas a few minutes later and called the paramedics. He was rushed to the emergency room of the local hospital, where he was diagnosed as suffering from panic anxiety with adrenaline fatigue brought on by too much stress. His symp-toms were those of a fairly classic anxiety-induced panic attack. This problem doesn't always show up on tests for adrenal func-tioning because the values for "normal" range so widely, but it shows itself quite clearly in the victim's sudden inability to tolerate stress or raise any energy in response to a demand.

For Thomas it has been a long struggle back to health. His profound fatigue limited his activity—including physical activity—for many months. Any kind of exertion, including mild exercise, would increase the lactate level in his blood and send him into a panic attack with strange body sensa-tions and fears.

Now, several years later, Thomas is almost his old self again, except that I hope through therapy with me, he has learned to live a more balanced life. He assures me that he "stops to smell his roses," listens to the birds in his garden, and takes time to fish.

Any of the following symptoms should be taken as a sign of impending anxiety attack or adrenaline exhaustion:

- *intense depression* of short duration (say, three days to one week) that occurs every few months
- unusual *difficulty in getting energy going* in the morning
- being *overcome by great tiredness* whenever there is a "let down"
- *strange body sensations* (tingling up and down the arms or across the chest) or strange aches in the joints and muscles
- *exhaustion* that occurs very easily or frequently
- *feelings of panic* triggered by activity or exercise

MILD FORMS OF STRESS FATIGUE

Most of us, I suspect, get caught up in crazy work schedules or unreasonable work demands from time to time. But most of us don't experience the dramatic form of stress exhaustion Thomas went through (although such an experience is certainly possible for all of us under conditions of extreme and prolonged stress).

Much more common is a milder form of adrenaline fatigue which is not as serious as the kind of major attack Thomas suffered. Nevertheless, it can have a significant negative impact on the quality of our lives.

What are some of the milder and less serious consequences of moderate stress fatigue?

* *chronic muscle tension* resulting in sore neck, shoulders and back, as well as common tension headaches
* *disturbance of the digestive system* resulting in chronic diarrhea, colitis, diverticulitis, ulcers, or constipation
* *chronic sleeplessness,* including difficulty falling asleep or waking up very early
* *persistent fatigue*—especially waking up tired every morning
* *loss of enthusiasm for life,* lack of excitement or interest in normal activities

THE CURE FOR ADRENALINE FATIGUE

The remedy for *all* forms of adrenal fatigue is learning how to manage your arousal so as to allow for adequate recovery time after periods of high adrenaline excitement. This, of course, also means learning to control your addiction to adrenaline because this addiction causes you to crave the "high" it creates.

By carefully evaluating the symptoms of addiction and fatigue and by heeding the warning inherent in all symptoms, we can *turn our bad stress into good.* Effective relaxation, improved sleeping habits, and, yes, even attention to our spiritual development and values will aid us in this quest for a balanced life. In the remainder of this book, I will be discussing specific techniques for achieving this balance.

Adrenaline and Cholesterol

Nothing I have to say in this book is as important and far-reaching as about how adrenaline and stress disease are connected. This topic is especially important because it shows how adrenaline affects the cardiovascular system. Report after report in both popular and professional literature has blamed cholesterol for the rampaging coronary artery disease of our day. But these reports almost totally ignore the role of adrenaline arousal in elevating cholesterol. Consequently, millions of Americans are being deluded into thinking that if their cholesterol level is within certain "normal" limits, they are safe from a potential heart attack.

B ut think again! The game of cardiovascular damage is played by *both* adrenaline and cholesterol, and the problem cannot be solved by paying attention to only one of the two.

The risk factors for heart disease most commonly highlighted in the popular press are cigarette smoking, high blood pressure, high blood cholesterol levels, diabetes, lack of exercise, obesity, and, lastly but thankfully, stress. But while such a list gives some recognition to the stress factor, use of the term "stress" in this literature almost always denotes trauma, tension, or anxiety—the unpleasant or catastrophic aspects of our existence. If you get fired from your job, you're considered to be under stress. If you are going through a divorce, the stress level is obvious. But as I have already shown, *stress is not confined to the gainful aspects of life*. It is very much a part of every demand or arousal—pleasant or unpleasant. And the role this kind of stress plays in causing heart disease depends on one's cholesterol level.

Simply put, if blood cholesterol levels are high, stress will much more likely contribute to heart disease than if it were low. On the other hand, if stress levels are kept low, even a high cholesterol level will *probably not* result in heart disease.

You see, adrenaline and cholesterol work in mutual dependency. The one uses the other to do the essential damage of depositing fatty plaque in the arteries of the heart. And one without the other is relatively harmless as far as your heart is concerned, all other factors being equal. But the two together can be deadly.

Now this is not to say that one should ignore cholesterol levels. NOT AT ALL! If you have a high cholesterol reading, *get it attended to right away.* Just don't ignore your stress!

Furthermore, there *are* other factors that can contribute to heart disease as well, so I'm not suggesting a simple one-to-one relationship. But the fact remains that the combination of prolonged adrenaline elevation and high cholesterol is a dangerous one as far as the heart and arteries are concerned.

UNDERSTANDING CHOLESTEROL

But what is cholesterol, anyway? Is it a poison? The way we speak of it, you would swear it was toxic. Should it be totally eliminated from our bodies? The answer is "No." We probably wouldn't survive many crises without it. Cholesterol is not in our bodies by accident, but serves an important function in our survival.

Although it has the connotation of being something harmful, cholesterol—like adrenaline—has a positive function in our bodies. In fact, it is indispensable for the maintenance of the body. Its *main function* is to contribute to the building up of cell membranes. It also serves as the basis for bile acids in the liver and for certain hormones.

Eighty to 90 percent of the body's total cholesterol is manufactured by the liver. The rest we get from the foods we eat.

Cholesterol is a soapy substance not soluble in water, which is where all the trouble starts. To become soluble so as to circulate through the bloodstream, it connects up with protein molecules to form compounds called *lipoproteins.* There are two different forms of lipoproteins with different ratios of protein to cholesterol. There are *high-density lipoproteins* (called simply HDLs) and *low-density* ones (LDLs).

When a doctor tells you your "cholesterol level," she usually is referring to the *total blood cholesterol level.* But this number tells you nothing about the relative amounts of HDLs and LDLs. And the difference is crucial, because research has shown that it is the LDLs that tend to increase the risk for heart disease, while HDLs lower the risk.

One other thing research has indicated is that higher circulating adrenaline seems to increase the amount of LDLs in the bloodstream—so now you can see the dangerous connection between adrenaline and cholesterol!

LOWERING CHOLESTEROL DOES HELPS

For more than thirty years, a debate has raged over whether or not lowering cholesterol levels really helps lower the risk of heart and artery disease. I believe the issue has finally been settled. In January 1984, the National Health, Lung, and Blood Institute released the findings of a ten-year, $150 million study of the incidence of heart disease among 3,806 middle-aged American men. *All* the subjects had high cholesterol levels when the research began, and they were followed very closely throughout the ten years of the study.

In what must be the most important medical news of the last two decades, the Institute reported that direct, overwhelming evidence now exists that reducing cholesterol levels *prevents heart attacks* and the likelihood of heart-attack deaths.

The study showed that for every 1 percent drop in cholesterol level, there is a 2 percent decrease in the risk of heart attack. When the cholesterol level was reduced 25 percent, the incidence of heart disease fell 50 percent. Over the ten years of the study, those who were on both low cholesterol diets and drugs had 24 percent fewer fatal heart attacks than those who did nothing to control cholesterol levels. This evidence is impressive and has been consistently replicated since. It conclusively shows that lowering one's blood cholesterol level is crucial for avoiding heart disease. But how low should cholesterol be? Much lower than hitherto believed, according to *Science Digest,* which quotes Dr. William Castelli, the director of the famous Framingham Heart Study involving five thousand residents of a Boston suburb:

> "Half the heart-attack victims in America have a cholesterol level between 150 and 250, but because their total cholesterol is under 250 (the one time acceptable limit of normal), they are being completely ignored by physicians. You see, if your cholesterol level is under 150 you are not going to have a heart attack—even if you smoke, have hypertension, and all the other stuff."[1]

What this indicates is that although any reduction in cholesterol levels is helpful, to be completely safe from the ravages of coronary artery disease it is necessary to cut the cholesterol level far below the amounts previously considered "normal." And the catch is that the commonly accepted ways of lowering cholesterol, namely diet, are insufficient to lower cholesterol to a level that is really safe! One needs to rely on the powerful cholesterol lowering medications now available.

DIET, DRUGS, AND EXERCISE ARE NOT ENOUGH

The most common "natural" recommended way of controlling blood cholesterol is through diet. Much has been written about this over the past few decades. The recommendations of the National Health, Lung, and Blood Institute study are straightforward and familiar:

- Cut down on saturated fats and high-cholesterol foods (lists of appropriate foods are widely available).
- Substitute fish and poultry for high-cholesterol red meats whenever possible.

- Eat only two or three eggs a week.

- Limit shellfish and organ meats such as liver to small portions each month.

- Cook with low-cholesterol vegetable fats (such as corn oil, olive oil, or safflower oil, and margarine made from such oils instead of saturated animal and vegetable fats (such as butter or coconut oil).

It is recommended that each person limit himself or herself to fewer than 300 milligrams of cholesterol per day. Since most of us consume more like 400–600 milligrams, the amount we eat should probably be halved.

But there is a catch when it comes to controlling cholesterol only through diet. The National Health, Lung, and Blood Institute study showed that change in diet was only able to bring about a 4 percent lowering of the level of cholesterol in the individuals studied. (Other studies put the figure at 10 or 11 percent.) This means that if your blood cholesterol level is, say, 250 milligrams per 100 milliliters (abbreviated simply as mg%), even a drastic change in diet would lower it about 10 mg%—to about 240 mg%. Not much of an improvement, especially in view of the recent evidence that cholesterol level should be far below the commonly accepted norm of 250 milligrams. Remember, only about 10 percent of our blood cholesterol comes from food, anyway; the majority is produced by the liver.

There are drugs available that lower cholesterol, and these can be very important for high-risk individuals. More and more physicians are prescribing these medications as a quick and effective way of reducing cholesterol. If your physician recommends this approach, don't hesitate. But even a combination of low-cholesterol diets and drugs may not sufficiently lower your cholesterol.

Exercise is another frequently cited way of lowering the risk of heart attack. Actually, regular exercise appropriately tailored to your age and level of fitness is helpful for almost everything. Self-esteem, mood, as well as physical health and cholesterol levels seem to benefit from regular physical exercise. So will your family, because it improves disposition as well!

Do you recall that a very famous runner dropped dead of a heart attack some years ago? He had even written several books about the benefits of running. But his hours on the track were not enough to prevent fatal coronary artery disease. While heredity probably played a significant role in this man's heart disease, his is not an isolated case. Enough people drop dead on running tracks every year to show that exercise itself is not enough to prevent heart attacks. *Something more is needed.*

ADRENALINE IS THE OTHER PART OF THE PICTURE

I believe that much of the current literature concerning cholesterol and heart disease fails to take into consideration the close connection between high cholesterol, stress, and adrenaline arousal. This, in my opinion, is the *missing link* often ignored when it comes to preventing heart disease.

An increase in circulating cholesterol during stress is part of the body's reaction to threatening stimuli. Coupled with this elevation, or perhaps resulting from it, is a corresponding elevation of adrenaline. The rise in cholesterol and adrenaline levels raises blood pressure and increases the circulation of blood to tissue where it is most needed.

There is abundant evidence that stress raises cholesterol levels. Accountants' cholesterol levels have been found to be highest at tax time; medical students register 10 percent higher during examination time; employees fired from their jobs show a 10 percent drop in cholesterol when they finally secure new work.[2]

Emotional upsets such as fear, anxiety, depression, and anger can be shown to raise both adrenaline and cholesterol levels. Depression especially has a marked effect, particularly on adrenaline, as does general emotional instability. A recent report shows that about 50 percent of those suffering from prolonged major depression have enlarged adrenal glands. Precisely what this means is still being debated, but it must at least mean that depression is a significant stressor!

As far as personality characteristics are concerned, two "dimensions" have been found to be associated with elevated cholesterol:

- *overactivity* (excessive competition, aggression, and impatience)
- *over control* (exaggerated sense of responsibility, conformism, and low self-esteem)

Both these personality traits are associated with the Type-A behavior pattern, which is known also to produce higher levels of adrenaline. Another psychological factor contributing to the recruitment of cholesterol appears to be that of "perceived helplessness." It appears from recent research that when a person is caught up in a situation about which he or she feels helpless and has no control over the outcome, cholesterol as well as adrenaline levels increase significantly. For the Type-A person who already has high levels of these two substances, the aggravation only increases the risk.

CONTROLLING CHOLESTEROL AND ADRENALINE

What does all this mean when it comes to preventing heart disease?

First of all, since blood cholesterol levels, adrenaline levels, and heart disease are closely linked, it is important to have your blood cholesterol tested regularly. Such a test should include determining the ratio of LDLs to HDLs, not just the combined total level. It is recommended that blood cholesterol be *checked every five years* or so after age twenty or twenty-one. Your physician will advise you as to what normal levels should be—but push for a "conservative" recommendation to be on the safe side.

Second, it is a good idea to maintain a blood cholesterol level that is well below what is usually considered the norm. This can be achieved to a certain extent by diet, medication, if necessary, and moderate exercise, but it also involves controlling adrenaline levels along the lines I will outline in later chapters.

This brings me to the third point, the one most crucial to this book: We must also educate ourselves in better stress management so as to reduce the damage that our stress hormones can cause in the presence of even slightly elevated cholesterol. In other words, *adrenaline management* cannot be separated from *cholesterol control.*

A recent survey by the same National Institute that conducted the cholesterol study, showed that only 39 percent of the physicians surveyed then believed that lowering cholesterol would help prevent heart disease.[3] The percentage is much lower now, I am sure, but with managed care running the show, it is possible to encounter resistance to preventative treatment. It won't be ignorance that avoids the treatment of slightly elevated cholesterol levels, but cost containment. Many of us will be forced to consider "natural" ways of self-treatment, and the models I am presenting here certainly don't cost anything if carefully followed.

Lowering adrenaline in the blood, whether by relaxation or psychological means and not just through medication, WILL lower the risk of heart disease. And lowering the adrenaline level will also contribute to the lowering of your cholesterol level.

So it is clear that adrenaline management and cholesterol management must remain closely linked. Both together are far more effective in preventing heart disease than either alone. In Part Three of this book I will look more closely at specific techniques for adrenaline management.

CHOLESTEROL AND YOUR CHILD

Since many of my readers are bound to be parents (or perhaps you have nieces or nephews), a few comments on how cholesterol affects children may be appropriate.

Controlling the eating habits of children, especially teenagers, these days is no easy task. High-calorie, high-fat junk food seems to be universally the preferred fare for anyone not yet able to earn their own keep! Parents should, therefore, be most concerned about how this affects the cholesterol levels of their children.

Is there a problem here? There most certainly is! The eating habits you instill in your children now can have a lifetime benefit for them. The same applies to stress control.

Research has shown that when children between the ages of eight and eighteen with high cholesterol levels were examined as adults, 43 percent were still having high cholesterol levels. Learning the basics of good nutrition, together with establishing proper lifestyles and attitudes toward stress, can make a big difference in adulthood!

We may not be able to control the genes we pass on to our offspring, but a healthy home can teach many profitable lessons and lead to healthy habits that will survive for a lifetime.

CONCLUDING REMARKS ON COMPETITIVE EXERCISE

Before going on to other topics, I would like to add a warning when it comes to diet and exercise as means of controlling cholesterol: Remember that stress and cholesterol are closely related. While exercise is good for everything, it is possible to become so intense and competitive in exercise that stress levels remain elevated instead of becoming depleted. Adrenaline can be recruited by challenge and excitement in exercise as easily as through trauma.

Instead of producing peace and relaxation, intense *competition* can make you frustrated and angry, and recruit high levels of adrenaline—even in basically healthy activities. You can run yourself into the ground every day and still not be protecting yourself from heart disease *if you maintain an* aggressive, over-competitive attitude, constantly racing against others . . . or even yourself.

"I'll be even better at staying on my diet today," or, "I'll show my boss—I can work even faster than he can") will continually trigger a "fight or flight" reaction with its attendant high cholesterol.

There is *only one way* to diet or exercise in a healthy, stress-lowering manner, and that is to avoid frustration, over-competitiveness, and hostility while you're doing it. That pretty well rules out Scotland's gift to the world—golf—for us beginners, doesn't it? Only joking, but as a beginning golfer I can see a lot of potential for stress ahead . . . *if* I take the game too seriously.

Reminds me of the golfer who said to his caddie, "Why do you keep looking at your watch?"

"It's not my watch," replied the caddie, "It's my compass!"

So before you golf, jog, cycle, ski on your Nordic Track®, do your pushups, or even eat your fish, do one important thing: make sure you are at peace with yourself and the world. It is my hope that the suggestions in this book will help you do just that.

Finding the Source of Your Stress

There was a time when people knew what stressed them. Life was simple and decisions relatively easy. "Should I eat or should I hunt? Should I find firewood or should I gather berries? I think I'll go to sleep!"

Occasionally, however, the pursuit of a small animal through the jungle brought an ancient hunter face-to-face with stress in the form of a saber-toothed tiger. Instantly the hunter's stress response system went into action. Adrenaline surged in the hunter's body to get the muscles primed and the nerves steeled for action. Now the decision that pressed for attention became: "Should I fight or should I run for my life?" The hunter's heart pounded in his chest and his breathing quickened as he looked intently at the eyes of his adversary, trying to discern its intent.

Tense moments passed. But apparently the beast wasn't hungry. After a quick snarl to assert its belief that it was the superior one, the saber-toothed tiger turned and slinked slowly away, vanishing into the shadows.

The crisis was over. The stress was past. Only the hunter's hungry stomach growled its disappointment.

MODERN JUNGLES

The days when we needed the courage to confront saber-toothed tigers are long gone, of course, but for many the modern jungle is just as dangerous. Perhaps it is even more so, because today's tigers are not as easily recognized and dealt with. Their stripes are less recognizable. They hide on crowded buses, crouch next to us on overnight plane connections, and snarl at us over scratchy telephones. Beasts, all right . . . but of a different sort!

There are many of these new beasts, and they can set the heart racing and the ears pounding far more readily than the slinky, feline kings of the jungle.

Unfortunately, our body's emergency system *was* designed for four-legged jungle hunts and not traffic jams . . . ferocious cats that occasionally confront us, then slink away, not neighbors who stay put. We are better equipped to meet challenges that require physical rather than psychological skill!

June knows the modern jungle well. Each day she sees it down in the valley below, just outside her bedroom window. A tall forest of concrete lurks, enveloped in a dingy cloud of smog. On the way into the jungle, she must maneuver through jungle-like tracks stalked by reckless drivers both behind and in front of her. The roar of honking horns is deafening and her heart races. Her teeth hurt from being clenched, and no amount of underarm deodorant can cope with the flood of perspiration. Her saber-toothed tiger wears a red-striped tie most days and growls instructions and grunts dissatisfactions through expensive orthodontically shaped "sabers." The boss prefers dishing out disappointments like, "Sorry, I must postpone your vacation," instead of scratching her arms with his claws.

What is the source of June's stress? It is everywhere and in everyone, it seems to her. There is no one source she can point to and say, "This—this alone is the source of my stress. If only I can take care of this one demand, all stress will be gone forever." She can't "run" out of her jungle because she doesn't know which direction is safest. She can't stop and "fight" because she's not sure who her enemy really is. The modern jungle is too big, too powerful, too complex, too confusing for her to make any sense of it.

So June sits behind her desk, day after day, stomach churning and pumping out acid, her back muscles knotting. She reaches for the "berries" of her jungle—two aspirin and some Maalox. If you can't beat it, at least try to numb it!

THE MANY SOURCES OF STRESS

There are many experts today who are concerned over the "stress epidemic" in our culture. Almost every direction you look, warning signs are up. Immunologists warn us that stress is damaging our immune systems, cardiologists warn of heart disease, cancer specialists declare that stress aggravates cancer. Dr. Joel Elkes of the University of Louisville says, "Our mode of life itself, the way we live, is emerging as today's principal cause of illness."[1]

He is absolutely right. It is not just Exxon tigers or Izod alligators that are our stressors, but every turn of each normal day. This makes it very much more difficult to pinpoint the source of stress. It is camouflaged by subtle shadows of normality and stripes of respectability. And if we don't know the source of our stress, there is no way we will be able to fight it. We have to know where our enemy is before we can remove it.

STRESSORS THAT EASILY ELUDE RECOGNITION

There can be many sources of stress that elude recognition in the average person's life, and I will discuss some of these shortly to help you see a little more clearly where yours comes from. Before I do, however, I want to emphasize again the importance of not looking for your stress only in the calamities of life. While major life changes such as divorce, death of a spouse, or losing a job certainly generate stress, the greater source of stress for most of us is to be found in those life issues that can best be called "minor hassles." There is a growing body of evidence that the everyday, minor annoyances of life contribute as much, if not more, to stress disease than major life traumas. They are certainly more prevalent! The panic of getting ready every morning for work or bickering with a rebellious teenage son or daughter may be as damaging as getting fired. If we don't watch these day-to-day minor hassles, they can eventually kill us.

How can we know if these everyday sources of stress are getting to us? I have devised a brief test (Figure 5) that might help pinpoint them for you. Answer the questions on it as honestly as you can, then add up your score according to the directions. See Appendix for how to interpret the results.

Figure 5

EVERYDAY HASSLES TEST

Give yourself one point for each "No" answer on questions 1 to 5, and one point for each "Yes" answer on questions 6 to 10.

	Yes or No	Score
1. Are you friendly toward *all* your neighbors and work colleagues?	____	____
2. Do you, on a daily basis, enjoy your world?	____	____
3. Do you feel financially secure?	____	____
4. Does life seem meaningful most of the time?	____	____
5. Do you feel in control of your life?	____	____
6. Must you combine housekeeping or parenting with having to earn a living?	____	____
7. Are you a single parent?	____	____
8. Do you feel angry toward someone or irritated by something at least once a day?	____	____
9. Do you often have sleepless nights—more than once a week?	____	____
10. Are you always in a hurry?	____	____
TOTAL		____

UNCOMMONLY RECOGNIZED STRESSORS

The more we know about where our stress comes from, the easier it will be for us to deal with. Hidden or unrecognized stress is the most damaging of all: it tends to create more fear than is appropriate for the amount of danger we actually face.

What are some hidden stressors—some less obvious sources of stress that we often overlook? In this chapter, I want to examine two of the most common: *people* and *pain*. In Part Three, I will suggest some positive ways to handle the stress that comes from these sources.

PEOPLE

I would guess that 95 percent of all stress originates with other people. The reason is obvious: We can't avoid people! It is people with whom we must live and to whom we must relate. People are our bosses, relatives, friends, colleagues, strangers, fellow church members, employees, tax collectors, and the police—and all can be sources of stress.

Why do people stress us? One reason is because we need them so much! We all have a need to be loved and accepted by others, and many of us will go to almost any length to achieve respect or avoid criticism. We fear rejection because we so desperately want to be thought of as having value. Our egos crave the respect of others.

At the same time, these people we need are inconsistent, unpredictable, and often more concerned about their own acceptance. They can be loving or generous, but they can also be inconsiderate, selfish, self-seeking, and self-satisfied. They don't always follow through on promises; they break commitments at the bat of an eye. We learn by experience that few people can be trusted entirely, and some appear to have an outright intent to harm us.

I don't mean to be cynical here. My intent is not to degrade all of human nature, but merely to highlight how difficult it is to live in a world that is basically imperfect, in a culture that is so super-individualistic, and filled with fellow humans as imperfect AS WE ARE!

In short, people cause us stress because everyone is just like us—human! And that can be a real source of stress. The better our people-relating skills, the lower our stress, by and large. The poorer our people-relating skills, the greater our stress will eventually become. It is not cars on our highways that cause us stress, but the *people* who drive them. It is not the *paper* on which threatening letters are written that causes us panic, but the intent and words of the *person* who means us harm.

How do people cause us stress? Chiefly they make us fearful and angry, by threatening our security or withholding the love or approval we crave. And the emotions of fear and anger, which in turn cause more fear and bring out self-protecting instincts, push buttons at the very core of our survival mechanisms. When we become angry or fearful, the message we send our bodies is "Danger!" And our bodies are designed to respond by releasing adrenaline. (In chapter 10, I will present some specific ways to deal with the stress produced by the "adrenaline-charged emotions" of anger and fear.)

Another reason why people stress us so much is that a great many of us have not learned, either in school or by the experiences of our lives, how to cope with the inconsistencies and inadequacies of others. Many of us lack adequate assertiveness and find it difficult to claim our basic rights as humans, either at work or in the home. There are basic, simple rights, such as the right to be heard, to be treated with respect, to be able to get what we pay for, to say what we feel, or to say "No" when we really don't want to do something.

If you cannot be adequately and lovingly assertive, then don't be surprised if you frequently feel stressed out. Under-assertiveness is the primary cause of much of the helplessness everyone feels from time to time. I think I am finally getting to the place in my life where I honestly do believe that I can be assertive without fearing the wrath of God descending upon me in the form of another person's anger.

Others of us lack the courage to be ourselves. Perhaps we don't even know what "being ourselves" means. "Who am I? What am I?"—these questions lie buried beneath much of our tension.

"If I really try to be my real self," we fear, "no one will like me." So we become what we *think* others want us to be. And this can be particularly stressful because we are only second-guessing what we think others would like us to be.

Pain

The stress produced by pain is very often overlooked. Unless they have experienced severe pain themselves—and I don't mean an everyday headache or cut finger—most people have no idea how much stress pain can produce. Pain is even harder to bear when we're not sure why we must suffer it in the first place.

I have been relatively free of pain most of my life. I once underwent some surgery, no life-threatening problem, but it did involve some muscle cutting and a "patch" to hold some bits and pieces in place because I had neglected to have the problem taken care of earlier. And my surgeon assured me that I could have the surgery under the "day surgery" arrangement, in which a patient checks into the hospital early in the morning, has the surgery, and leaves the same afternoon.

The surgeon's words to me were, "You might as well go home—and suffer there, because you will be in a lot of pain afterwards." Well, dear man that he is, he didn't tell me how *painful* "a lot of pain" is, and he forgot—or avoided—to tell me how long it would last. I have never appreciated how beneficial an effective pain-killer can be as I did the first week after my surgery. Thank God for analgesics!

Now, I know that what I experienced was petty compared with some pain sufferers I have known. But it helped me to discover that my previous absence of real pain (even when I nearly severed a finger as a child) had misled me into believing that pain is really not all that bad! Ignorant me!

During the first week after my surgery I carried out an experiment. I tested my urine for stress hormones. I measured my cholesterol levels. I monitored my skin temperature on biofeedback instruments and checked for other physical indicators of stress. The results confirmed what I already knew—pain produces the most intense stress reactions. And if the pain continues for a long period of time, as with certain chronic disorders such as arthritis, it will produce stress disease just as surely as will a hurried lifestyle.

Our knowledge of the neurophysiology and psychology of pain is presently undergoing a dramatic expansion. While we haven't solved the all-important question of the *meaning of pain*, the knowledge we have accumulated is helping us provide a little more relief for those who must bear more of it than they deserve. In chapter 10, I will provide a few suggestions for making pain less stressful.

ANALYZING YOUR STRESSFUL WORLD

Whether your stress is produced by pleasant or painful life events, or by people or unfortunate life circumstances, the *source of your stress* must be clearly identified before you can take the next step of effectively managing the adrenaline that is triggered by it.

To help you pin-point the source of stress, I have devised a simple system of record-keeping that you should use as often as possible over the next few weeks.

Examine Figure 6. Make several photocopies for your use. For a period of one week at a time, closely observe your daily activities. Every time you feel bothered, worried, angry, excited, or stirred up in any way, place a small check mark next to the category listed. (You may have to make very small marks for some of the items because they will occur often! There won't be enough space if you don't keep your writing tiny.)

Notice that there are four major environments that make up your life: home, work, recreation/church, and general. There is extra space for you to add any other category or specific situation.

At the end of the week, total up the number of marks against each specific event, and you will begin to see where the source of your stress really lies. You may be in for some surprises. I've kept a record like this many times, and each time I have been amazed at how a particular life event can cause stress over and over again, yet continually elude recognition.

When you have identified your major stressor or stressors, you can more intelligently begin to plan a strategy for coping with them. And that is what the last section of this book is all about.

Figure 6

ANALYZING YOUR STRESSFUL ENVIRONMENT

Period: _____ to _____ (one week at a time)
Check, as often as necessary, the appropriate experiences as they occur.
Add any experiences personal to yourself.

HOME:	Checks	Total
Angry at spouse		
Angry at children		
Sexual difficulty		
Financial problems		
Family conflict		
Too many demands		
Trouble with in-laws		
Illness in family		
Major loss		
Blaming or projecting		
Houseguests or lodgers		
Remodeling or construction		
Wedding, divorce, etc		

RECREATION/CHURCH:	Checks	Total
Could not relax		
Loneliness		
Destructive habits		
Inadequate exercise		
No support		
Interpersonal conflict		
No responsibilities		
Too many responsibilities		
Physical training		
Spiritual "awakening"		
Stimulating relationships		

WORK:	Checks	Total
Angry at boss		
Angry at fellow workers		
Making mistakes		
Noise irritants		
Too much work to do		
Too little work to do		
Change in pay or hours		
Pressure of deadlines		
Poor time management		
Poor prioritizing		
Lack of assertiveness		
Challenging project		

GENERAL:	Checks	Total
Difficulty sleeping		
Angry at neighbors		
Criticized by another		
Problems with car		
Weather conditions		
Emotions cause problems		
Too much excitement		

How to Monitor Your Adrenaline Arousal

I consider this chapter to be at the heart of all I am communicating about stress management. As I have shown in previous chapters, the excessive flow of the stress hormones, especially adrenaline, is the essence of the stress response. The first step toward learning how to control the secretion of these hormones and thus reduce stress disease is to be able to recognize when you are being stimulated to produce more adrenaline. If you don't know when you are pumping adrenaline, you are not likely to be doing anything to control it.

But is adrenaline always bad? There are many situations in which high adrenaline arousal is appropriate. A demanding task or crisis requires all the energy we can muster. An occasional adrenaline "rush" is both pleasurable and life-enhancing. Games would be no fun if we didn't get a surge of excitement at winning or a desire to get revenge and win back the trophy we have lost. Yes, high adrenaline does have some positive value.

But many of us have become adrenaline abusers. We employ more adrenaline for a given task than is really necessary by "psyching" ourselves up to it. So, knowing *when to allow arousal and when to switch it off* is essential for effective stress management. A long and healthy life depends on it! If we know when we are producing high levels of adrenaline, we can exercise our freedom to choose whether we want it to continue. We can decide that we need the adrenaline and let it continue to do its work, or we can decide to conserve our energy and therefore slow down the adrenaline response. We *do* have the ability to control our adrenaline, primarily through taking control of our thinking and targeting relaxation.

It's all a matter of choice. But we can only make intelligent choices if we know when our adrenaline is aroused.

My purpose, therefore, is to teach you how to monitor your adrenaline arousal, so you can manage it to your best advantage.

THE SIGNS OF ADRENALINE AROUSAL

To be able to monitor adrenaline arousal requires that you first understand the effects that adrenaline produces in the body. Let's review the sequence of events from the moment we perceive a threat or challenge to the point at which our insides are bathed in adrenaline.

In response to a stressor, chemical messages are sent by the brain through the pituitary gland and nervous system to the adrenal glands (refer to Figure 1, chapter 3). The release of stress hormones by the adrenal glands produces the following physical changes that are in one way or other measurable changes:

- increase in heart rate
- increase in blood pressure
- decrease in size of arteries and capillaries in hands and feet (peripheral vasoconstriction)
- increase in muscle tension.

There are many other changes, but they are not as readily observed as these four. And it is the relative ease of measuring these reactions that makes it possible for us to *monitor* our adrenaline arousal (and thus the level of our stress) on an ongoing basis.

Of particular interest from this standpoint is the constriction of the blood vessels in the hands and feet. This constriction happens partly because blood is needed more in other parts of the body, such as the heart and lungs, and so the arteries and capillaries decrease in size to reduce circulation.

But this constriction also serves to protect us from bleeding to death should we cut ourselves during the "fight or flight" response. The observable result is that the temperature of the hands—particularly the fingers—drops. This is commonly experienced as *cold hands*, a reaction of fear, anxiety, or excitement. No doubt you have felt this response often.

Because the temperature of the fingers can be so easy to measure, with or without a thermometer, it provides a convenient sign for the presence of stress, and I will be concentrating on it as a primary way of measuring adrenaline arousal. But it is also possible, with a little training, to monitor your heart rate, blood pressure, and muscle tension, which together give a very reliable indication of stress—especially when you are, in fact, enjoying the experience. While these are a little more cumbersome, they can be very helpful in getting a more complete picture of your body's stress response.

THE PURPOSE OF ADRENALINE MONITORING

Why bother with discovering when you are stressed? You need to be aware of your adrenaline arousal so that you can:

- better understand how your body responds to stress;
- be alert to particular stressful events in your life;
- increase the awareness of your freedom to choose;
- decide whether or not you want to be adrenally aroused;
- establish a baseline from which you can tell whether you are becoming more stressed than before;
- tell whether you are beginning to be master over your stress.

Why is it important to be able to measure your level of stress? Because stress is elusive and slippery. Those who are most stressed are also the ones least likely to be aware of their stress. They tend to deny that they are stressed. It isn't until they suffer severe pain or discomfort from their overstress that they begin to take notice. And even then, the tendency is to deny the stress and remove the pain by taking painkillers or antacids. Objective evidence of stress is much harder to ignore!

Effective monitoring requires that you get into the habit of taking the various measurements I will describe. At first, this should be done hourly. If this sounds time consuming, it isn't really. Adrenaline monitoring takes only a few minutes and quickly becomes almost second nature. Before long you will be monitoring your stress without giving it much thought. Once you have established an adequate "baseline" from which comparisons can be made, and once you have developed a clear sense of how your system responds to stress, you can ease up on the frequency of your monitoring and take only one or two measurements during the day or during stressful periods. Of course, the higher the level of your stress, the more frequently you will need to measure your response. If your early measurements show you are not very stressed, then less frequent measurements will be sufficient.

There is one important condition for a successful, self-taught stress management program: *Be honest with yourself at all times.* It is not a sign of weakness to acknowledge that you are over-stressed. In fact, the strongest among us are frequently the ones under the most pressure. But it takes courage and maturity to be willing to admit that you may have a problem with the way you respond to that pressure.

METHODS FOR FACTORING ADRENALINE AROUSAL

The following methods are all helpful in discovering how your body responds to stress. If you have questions about any of them, be sure to ask your doctor.

MEASURING HEART RATE

Your heart rate can be measured in a number of simple ways, no matter where you are—at work or play. You can use one of the fancy new electronic devices designed for joggers and exercise buffs. I have a wrist watch that makes the task a breeze. These are portable, accurate, and easy to use; you place your finger into or on a special sensor, then read your heart rate on the display. In meetings, on the train or plane . . . anywhere . . . you can instantly know how much work your heart is doing.

But why use expensive instruments? It's not hard to measure your heart rate the old-fashioned way—with your finger on your pulse. Simply place one or two fingers (not your thumb) on the artery at your wrist. A little searching about between the ligaments of your wrist will help you find it. Or, if you prefer, you can find the pulse in your neck, just under your jaw. Don't press too hard or you might cut off the blood flow to your brain, and this could be a problem! Count the pulses while you observe the second hand on a watch or clock. You need only count for fifteen seconds, then multiply by four.

Take your pulse often and write your pulse rate down in a notebook together with a description of where you are and what you are doing so you can observe how various situations affect you. It is very easy to tell when your adrenaline is aroused: Your pulse rate goes up. It may only go up a few beats—or it may jump up to a very fast rate. The degree of change is what counts.

You will notice that almost every time you take your pulse, it varies. This is normal because it changes constantly, sometimes increasing, sometimes slowing, in response to the many signals your heart receives from your adrenaline. Observe what makes it go faster and what slows it down. After awhile, you will get so used to the time interval between beats that you need merely place your finger on your pulse to instantly tell whether your heart is beating faster than normal.

But what is a *normal pulse rate?* That depends on many factors. Athletes have a slow rate; children and some elderly people have a faster one—and all are normal. If you are a typical, healthy person, your resting heart rate will probably be between seventy and seventy-five beats per minute. Generally speaking, the slower the better, although it is best to check with your doctor if you have any questions about what *your* heart rate should be.

For the purpose of adrenaline monitoring, find out what your pulse rate is *when you are totally relaxed*. The best time is before you get out of bed in the morning. This gives you your lowest, baseline resting pulse rate. Knowing what it is gives you a base for comparing your rate at other times of day so you can immediately tell when you are experiencing an adrenaline surge.

BLOOD PRESSURE

While it is not as practical to carry around a phygmomanometer (the instrument that measures blood pressure), blood pressure nevertheless should be measured regularly. You should know what your average blood pressure is. Measuring blood pressure is important because it not only shows you when you are stressed, but also tells you when you are adapting upwards or downwards in response to your general arousal. In other words, blood pressure tells if the cumulative effects of stress are getting out of control.

If I have a bad day at the office or with my students, my heart rate will fluctuate up and down. By the end of the day, my heart rate may be normal, but my blood pressure may be up—indicating that the stress of the day is still bothering me. It helps me to understand my overall response to the total stress I am experiencing.

But let me sound a warning: The mere act of measuring your own blood pressure can, at first, push it up quite high. Most of us are anxious about being "measured," and blood pressure can be very responsive to the fear of finding out that something is wrong. So don't pay too much attention to the first few readings you take. Just practice the measuring procedure repeatedly until you feel less threatened.

Many effective and simple-to-use blood-pressure instruments are now available at low cost. If you can afford it, buy one. If you can't, leave it alone and rely on the other measures I am describing. The best is the type that is "electronic" and doesn't use a stethoscope. When you pump up the "cuff," the instrument emits electronic "beeps" that can be counted. Some models even deflate the cuff automatically, so you can't botch the job too easily! Home-monitoring kits come with complete instructions, so I won't repeat them here. Practice until you can do it quickly and accurately and keep careful records. Your physician will gladly show you how to measure your blood pressure if you have difficulties.

The newer, smaller units now available to measure your blood pressure on your finger are very convenient. You can take them with you anywhere. But they are trickier to use and maintain valid readings, so follow the instructions carefully. I've recently been using a wrist watch that measures my blood pressure with very good results—but it's not everyone's cup of tea, as it takes some skill to set it up.

As with heart rate, you must establish a baseline from which to make comparisons. Measure your blood pressure every morning for a week and note the variations. This should help you determine your normal resting pressure. If it is above normal, see your physician. You may just be having a reaction to the measurement, but there is no point in ignoring it. Then regularly measure your pressure at other times and write down the readings, noting date and time.

A good time to measure your pressure is shortly after dinner when you've done your chores or put the kids to bed, then once more when you are in bed. It helps to be lying or sitting in the same place and in the same position each time so that you don't get differences due to postural factors.

What is a normal blood pressure? It depends on your age and physical condition. A reading of 120 over 80 is considered "normal" for most people. (The first figure is the "systolic," or *heart contraction*, pressure; the second is the "diastolic," or *heart resting* pressure.) A reading of 140 over 90 is generally considered to be the upper end of normal, provided you are resting and not having an adrenaline surge.

Consult your physician if you are at all concerned about your blood pressure, or if you want to know what your normal blood pressure should be. Elevated blood pressure is dangerous in the long run, so get professional help quickly if you think you need it. Treatment by diet and drugs is very effective in lowering blood pressure temporarily, but long-term treatment must also include a change in your lifestyle to find the best way of coping with stress. Even if your blood pressure is normal, you may want to think about these *before* you develop a problem with your blood pressure.

Finger Temperature

We now come to what may be the most fascinating—and certainly the easiest—measure of adrenaline arousal we currently have at our disposal: skin or finger temperature.

Do you remember how the "mood ring" craze swept through the country several years ago? These rings were supposed to tell the "mood" of the wearer by its changing colors. If the ring was blue, the wearer was supposedly in a good mood— happy and peaceful. If the stone turned black, the wearer was supposedly down, depressed, angry, and miserable. In between were green and yellow, meaning the wearer was emotionally "in between" moods.

Now, these rings actually had an element of truth behind them. They functioned on a very simple but valid principal: The skin's temperature, especially the fingers, goes up or down depending on what sort of reaction a person is having to a particular life event. Built into the surface of the ring was a temperature-sensitive liquid crystal that changed colors depending on the temperature of the hand. It was nothing more than a simple thermometer that measured the temperature of the skin.

But there were two things wrong with these mood rings. First, they did not measure "moods" at all, but adrenaline arousal! In other words, they measured stress response. Of course, there is often a connection between mood and stress level, and that's why the rings seemed to work—and sold millions.

Second, when exposed for too long to the atmosphere, they often measured air temperature rather than skin temperature. They certainly didn't work very well in extreme hot or cold weather!

The principle that the skin's temperature fluctuates in response to stress and arousal is now well-established. As I have indicated, this is called "peripheral vasoconstriction," and is a part of the body's protective system in response to stress.

What happens is this: In response to stress, nerve and hormonal signals (including adrenaline) are sent to the blood vessels in the hands, which then constrict and reduce the volume of blood present in the fingers. The skin, therefore, becomes colder as the flow of blood (which is warmer than the air) is restricted. Whereas blood temperature is 98.6°F, the air in a normal room will be about 72°F. If the blood vessels are completely relaxed, the temperature of the skin can go up to almost blood temperature, even in a cold room. A very relaxed person could, therefore, achieve a skin temperature of around 94°F or higher.

But when blood vessels constrict, the temperature drops and can go as low as room temperature if the reaction is severe.

This fluctuation of skin temperature goes on all the time. Relaxation makes skin warmer, and arousal makes it colder. For the most part, we don't feel these variations, because the brain blocks them out. Currently I am doing research, using a small instrument that can measure finger temperature throughout the day, for several days at a time. This way I can follow a patient into his or her real world and have a record of how stress affects them minute-by-minute. This should help to measure both stress proneness as well as the effectiveness of different treatments.

During stress, when adrenaline is increased, the drop in temperature of the hand can be measured quite readily. In recent years, little round plastic temperature dots have been developed that have liquid crystal embedded in them. These little dots change color in response to the change in skin temperature, just like mood rings used to do. By placing one of these dots (the back is coated with adhesive) on the hand in a non-intrusive position (see Figure 7), you can have a simple yet effective measure of moment-by-moment changes in your level of adrenaline arousal. Obviously, if you place your hands in cold water the dot will measure the temperature of the cold water. But if you remain in a stable room temperature, the dot will provide a convenient and accurate estimate of your skin temperature. As you will see, this can be a lifesaver!

If you are careful not to lose the dot and place it on a smooth plastic surface each time you take it off so as not to destroy the adhesive on the back, it will last you a long time. I keep one conveniently stuck on my watch dial. It also reminds me each

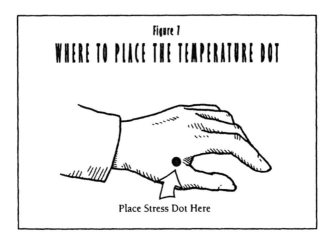

Figure 7

WHERE TO PLACE THE TEMPERATURE DOT

Place Stress Dot Here

time I look at my watch to *relax!* The temperature dots should not be exposed to water or placed in direct sunlight for very long.

To use a temperature dot, remove it from its paper backing and place it on the back of the left hand (right hand, if you are left-handed) in the web of skin between thumb and forefinger (see Figure 7).

Notice, as you do so, that the dot will immediately change color—assuming, of course, that you are not overstressed. If you are, it will probably remain black. The colors range from black to yellow to green to blue, starting at about 80°F and going up to above 90°F. With the temperature dot, you can estimate your skin temperature to within one or two degrees Fahrenheit. This isn't sensitive enough for clinical relaxation training, where we use instruments to measure skin temperature to an accuracy of one tenth of a degree or more, but it is sufficient for monitoring adrenaline arousal in real-life situations.

Almost any small thermometer held between the thumb and first finger, including the little alcohol thermometers found on desk calendars, will serve the same purpose as the dots. But measuring skin temperature with a thermometer is slightly more time-consuming and inconvenient.

What is a normal hand temperature? Ideally, one should try to relax so as to achieve a temperature over 90°F, preferably between 92 and 94°F. This can be done when you are in a normal air-conditioned room. If the room is colder, it may be difficult to warm up to this level. If it is too warm, the reading will be false.

During stress, some people only drop one or two degrees. Others can drop as much as twenty degrees and have hand temperatures as low as room temperature. By monitoring your skin temperature over a period of time, you will develop an understanding of your own unique responsiveness.

There are some factors other than stress that can affect the color of the dots, and it is helpful to keep this in mind to avoid false readings. Physical activity will lower the temperature and cause the color to change, as will raising your hand above your head (which drains blood away). If the room temperature is below 65°F (air-conditioning too high or during winter), it will be very difficult for your body to keep the hands warm. The body conserves its heat by withdrawing blood from the extremities. This is *not a stress response*, just the body's normal adaptive response to cold.

Cold hands are also found in chronic migraine sufferers, certain diseases of metabolism such as diabetes, and in the elderly, where blood circulation is often diminished. Raynaud's Syndrome, a disease of poor circulation, also causes cold hands. Excluding these factors, however, consistently cold hands should be taken as a sign of possible adrenaline over-arousal.

Interestingly, both migraine headaches and Raynaud's Syndrome are now treated by the use of biofeedback instruments which teach the patient to warm his or her hands. This equipment gives the patient signals corresponding to the temperature of the hand (hence the term *biofeedback,* which means "biological feedback"). The patient then learns ways to raise and lower hand temperature by reducing adrenaline arousal, and the generalized relaxation that this creates helps increase blood circulation and prevents the migraines. I often use the same technique in my clinical practice for stress and find it very effective. Since handwarming can only be accomplished by reducing adrenaline arousal, these biofeedback techniques can be very helpful for a wide variety of stress-related physical disorders.

Some people, notably those with Type-A behavior patterns and those who are prone to anxiety, have very "reactive" skin temperatures. In other words, their skin temperature changes often and shows large shifts up and down. Others tend to stay warm or cold all the time. By recording your temperature at hourly intervals throughout the day or during heavy or demanding work, you can get a clear picture of the stressful events that make up your day and how you respond to them. What you should do with this information is the subject of the next part of this book.

But first, let me tell you one more way to get a rough idea of your skin temperature without any fancy gadgets.

I am sure you have shaken hands with someone and then been told, "My, your hands are cold!" This most often happens when you are under stress. Many ministers and priests experience the "cold hands" reaction after preaching and are sometimes embarrassed when shaking hands with parishioners.

You can use this phenomenon to develop a simple test for adrenaline arousal. Since only the hands get cold under stress—not the face—you can place your hands on your cheeks and "take your temperature." If your hands feel colder than your cheeks, you are likely to be having an adrenaline surge. The greater the difference in temperature between hands and face, the greater the stress reaction. This method allows you to take your stress temperature at any time, in any place.

Muscle Tension

It is not easy to measure muscle tension without expensive equipment. In clinical biofeedback work, we use an instrument called an "electromyograph." If you are seeing a psychotherapist who provides biofeedback treatment, ask him or her to measure a few of your muscles to determine how tense you are. If not, the best alternative is to develop some skill at subjectively assessing your own muscle tension.

When you lie down at night, focus on each muscle group throughout your body and notice whether any of them feel tense. Do they feel "jumpy?" Is there pain anywhere? If there is, the feeling almost certainly means you are tense in the muscle where the pain is occurring.

Be alert for tightness in the stomach, discomfort in the chest, twitching in any part of the body, a feeling of tightness in the jaw muscles, or sensations in the head above the eyes or toward the back. These can all be signs of muscle tension. The relaxation techniques I will describe in chapter 11 can help you learn to lower your tension. Once you learn to recognize how it feels when your muscle tension is low, you can more easily tell when you begin to tense up.

PROFESSIONAL WAYS OF MEASURING ADRENALINE AROUSAL

In the event that you or someone close to you needs professional help, I would like to briefly summarize how adrenaline arousal can be measured by a physician or stress psychologist. Unfortunately, not much of what I will describe has moved out of the research laboratory into general clinical practice, so it is not widely known.

The self-help techniques I have just described will only provide you with a rough (though still very helpful) guide as to the extent of your stress level. To be more precise, it is necessary for biofeedback instruments to be used and for the level of adrenaline and other critical hormones in either your blood or urine to be measured directly. Cholesterol level is also important and its assessment should be included in a thorough check-up of your susceptibility to stress.

When measuring adrenaline, blood sampling is probably the first choice of the physician because blood adrenaline level most closely reflects the ongoing state of your stress response at the time of collection. But there is a disadvantage to this form of measurement. Because blood sampling techniques draw blood from a vein, many patients respond with increased anxiety during the procedure. This can easily elevate the level of adrenaline arousal and give a false positive stress reading. Blood levels of adrenaline do not, therefore, provide a foolproof way of measuring stress, except in chronic, persistent cases when the patient becomes accustomed to the procedure.

Fortunately, we have an easier solution in the analysis of urine for adrenaline. There is little or no anxiety associated with sampling urine, except for the inconvenience. And there is usually an abundant supply available. The procedure itself does not produce stress.

To avoid momentary stress reactions from giving a false reading, however, the preferred method of urine sampling is to have the patient collect in a sterilized bottle the total production of urine over a twenty-four-hour period, starting after the first voiding of the day. In this way, a sample of all the stress hormones secreted in the urine for a particular day's activities can be analyzed.

What is being measured in a urine analysis? The stress hormones produced by the outer layer of the adrenal glands, after circulating through the blood, are passed through the kidneys for recovery. A small percentage of adrenaline and other hormones (especially cortisol) escapes the kidney's recovery system and passes into the urine. The amount passed by unstressed patients is very small. But during times of excitement or stress, there is a great increase in the secretion of these hormones. The level of cortisol in the urine has thus become a popular choice for sensitively measuring the amount of physiological arousal a person is experiencing in response to stress.

If there is any question in your mind whether you need professional help in controlling your stress, I would urge you to contact your physician. He or she can advise you as to whether the procedures described above would be helpful or not and refer you, if necessary, to a specialist in the field of stress control and biofeedback.

Most people, however, can do a lot toward reducing their stress levels and healing their hurry sickness without seeking professional help. In the last section of this book, I want to show specific ways all of us can learn to manage the stress in our lives by using natural, rather than artificial means.

PART THREE

Healing Your "Hurry Sickness"

"Another aspect of the phenomenon is our present infatuation with speed. Having invented objects that can travel, communicate, or fabricate other objects at a greater and greater rate, we now seem willing to subject ourselves to their demands. Your great-grand-father, for example, trotting along in his horse-drawn buggy at a leisurely pace, might very well have stopped to chat with a passing neighbor for ten minutes or so. Encased in your car, you will be fortunate even to glimpse your neighbor as you each hustle by. . . .

Isn't there truth in the idea that the faster a machine is made to operate, the faster the operator feels he must think and act?"

—MEYER FRIEDMAN and RAY ROSENMAN
Type-A Behavior and Your Heart

Managing Your Adrenaline

As I have already described, it is the excessive flow of adrenaline and related stress hormones that is the essential factor in stress disease. Your program of stress management will not be effective, therefore, unless you learn to bring your adrenaline production under control.

Can you so control your secretion of adrenaline that, rather than it being the source of disease, you form an alliance with it? Definitely *yes*. By following a few simple procedures, you can live at peace with your stress. It can be your servant rather than your master. All it takes is a little perseverance and some understanding of how and when you arouse your adrenaline.

If you know when you are adrenally aroused, you can exercise your power of choice. You can choose whether or not you need the extra adrenaline, and then—if you don't need it—you may set about lowering it.

A word of encouragement: It is never too late to start controlling the over use of your body's defense system. Even if you are an "adrenaline addict" (and I was once) with advanced heart disease, or if you have already experienced a heart attack, you can prevent further damage and promote healing—even reverse some of the damage—by learning to manage the behavior that created the problem in the first place.

HOW MUCH ADRENALINE DO WE REALLY NEED?

Dave is a pastor—a very competent and greatly loved pastor. He cares about people, and they respond by flocking to his services and finding great joy in his ministry to them.

Dave is also an extraordinarily good preacher. He knows how to communicate, and his deep voice resonates across the pews.

But there is a problem in Dave's life. He is concerned about how excited he becomes when he preaches, so he has come to see me about it. He heard me talk about stress at a conference, and his concern shifted to real fear that he may be headed for trouble. Whatever he does, he "gives it his all," totally surrendering himself to the task before him. Afterward, he feels washed out, weighted beneath a profound exhaustion that he knows is not normal. After all, his work is not all that physical; he can't understand why he becomes so fatigued.

Often he has the feeling that he can't go another day, preach another sermon, or even answer one more ringing telephone— ever. The brief time he spends greeting parishioners after the last of his three Sunday morning services is absolute misery for him. He feels wrung out and drained dry, with nothing to say and little incentive to care. He longs for it all to be over so he can crash on the couch at home and hibernate for a few hours.

"What's wrong with me?" he asks pleadingly. "Am I experiencing some kind of spiritual depression? Am I losing it? I really think there's something wrong with me."

But Dave's is not a spiritual problem. He has become so accustomed to creating a "super-high," an adrenaline rush of massive proportions to accomplish the preaching task, that he literally exhausts his body's adrenal system. So it crashes when the last task is done. Furthermore, he has become a slave to insomnia, and this only makes his "ups" and "downs" worse.

The weekly extremes of "ups" and "downs" are beginning to take their toll on his mind, body, and spirit. To add insult to injury, he is developing a conditioned fear of the "letdown" which always follows his preaching. If he continues this way, he may be forced to leave the ministry! I've seen it happen often to clergy, lawyers, teachers, policemen, firemen—to those in any vocation where adrenaline flows to excess. The extremely sensitive human body will not be able to withstand this form of abuse indefinitely. I warned Dave about this after our first session together.

"I want you to let me teach you how to control and limit your use of adrenaline," I suggested to him. "You need to learn how to function at a lower level of arousal, at all times. You are using a bulldozer to do what a garden rake can do!"

Dave was flabbergasted. While he didn't fully understand the physiology of his abuse, he believed the only way he could preach effectively was to get "psyched up" to a high level of energy. He thought he would be considered a failure if he didn't come across with great intensity and verve. No one would pay attention; people would not be gripped by the message; he would just become like any other run-of-the-mill, dull preacher. These were his fears.

After explaining to him how his adrenal system worked, however, I finally persuaded him to *try* to preach with less intensity and a lower level of stimulation. I suggested the following: Instead of spending five or six hours each Saturday going over his sermon and "psyching" himself up, he was to relax and do something that would distract him from his sermon. This meant, of course, preparing his sermon earlier in the week.

Then, early Sunday morning, he was to skip the usual three cups of coffee to get himself going, and after his usual prayer time he was to take a casual walk to the church, which was about a mile away from his home. Rather than frantically reviewing sermon notes before the first service, he was to take ten minutes and do a deep muscle relaxation exercise, along the lines of the one described in chapter 11.

Dave was quite apprehensive the next Sunday, but he faithfully followed my prescription—if only to prove me wrong. He really believed *his* way was the *only* way! In the back of his mind, he was deathly afraid he would flop horribly—but he had the courage to try anyway.

I eagerly awaited our next therapy session. To his surprise, not mine, he felt so much more peaceful throughout the church service. His preaching, while not as physically energetic as before, deeply moved his congregation. They tracked with him better, had time to reflect on his comments to them, and didn't feel that everything was hectic. This was the feedback he got from a trusted friend afterwards. Best of all, after the three services were over, he felt like he still had some energy left—enough to actually enjoy moving among his parishioners to chat with them.

How much adrenaline do we need to perform any sort of work? In most situations, not very much—and usually less than we *think* we need! Little of what we do is actually life-threatening or in the nature of an emergency, and we only wound ourselves by reacting as if it were.

You may not have to preach every Sunday like Dave, and your life may be very routine or even boring, but you will have your equivalent periods of adrenaline demand:

- a deadline you must meet
- a neighbor who is antagonistic
- a child who is acting up
- a spouse who is seriously sick
- an elderly parent who needs care
- a program for some organization that needs planning
- a job that is not satisfying
- a lump that must be biopsied.

We all face challenges and upheavals that demand an "emergency" mode of response.

And how much adrenaline do we need in order to respond to these challenges? Again, not as much as we think. Stress can be aggravated by trying too hard. Most of us put forth too much effort for the task at hand. We overreact with fear to circumstances that are unusual.

Our brains would work better if we didn't panic. Our actions would be more effective if they were not so tense; if we spoke our orders quietly and didn't shout them. Our hearts would certainly be healthier if we kept our adrenaline levels down as much as possible. And we can choose for ourselves how much adrenaline we use. *It is possible* to bring our propensity for high arousal under control.

MONITORING ADRENALINE AROUSAL

In the previous chapter, I showed how to measure the adrenaline level. When facing a particularly demanding or challenging situation, the first step is to assess the level of your adrenaline arousal.

Take a moment to practice a self-monitoring exercise. Review your muscles for the telltale signs of tension. Are you clenching your jaw? What about your forehead or your neck? Do they feel tense? Are the muscles knotted and strained? To improve your ability to sense muscle tension, try tightening these muscles slightly and notice how they feel. Now relax them again . . . and notice the difference.

Observe your hands: Are they cold? They can turn blue before some of us pay attention! Test them against your face. Do they feel icy? If so, chances are your body thinks it is an emergency—assuming, of course, you're not outside playing in the snow!

Next, note your breathing. Does it seem shallow and fast? Can you hold your breath easily, or does trying to hold your breath make you feel panicky—as if you are compelled to breathe? If you have these feelings, you are probably hyperventilating—a sign that your adrenaline is very high.

Take your pulse. Is it slow and even? If it is faster than usual and you are not physically exerting yourself, chances are good that you are on an adrenaline kick.

DECIDE ABOUT YOUR ADRENALINE AROUSAL

By monitoring your adrenaline arousal in these ways, you can usually spot the early stages of an emergency response. When this happens, the next step is to ask yourself: *Do I need to be in a state of emergency right now?*

If the answer is *yes* (meaning you really *do* need a high level of adrenaline production), then go ahead and use all the adrenaline you can get going.

If your answer is *no*, this is not an emergency, then move quickly to relaxing your body and quieting your mind. No need to be afraid. You certainly don't need all that extra adrenaline. Staying calm and quiet will probably do more good for you at this point than being highly aroused.

Occasionally (and I mean *very occasionally*) you may not be sufficiently alert to respond to a demand. Perhaps due to fatigue, illness, or even depression, you just can't work up the energy you need to carry out your responsibilities. Then it may be appropriate—on a short-term basis only—to work at getting your adrenaline going by doing something physical or by thinking through the implications of not taking action. Here is one instance in which knowing how to "psych" yourself up may be useful!

How long should an adrenaline rush be allowed? This is the all-important question. It all depends on the circumstances. Let us suppose you are facing a crisis. On the way to an important meeting, your car has broken down. *Emergency!* your brain shouts subconsciously, and the adrenaline starts pumping. You move into high gear, find the nearest telephone, and decide who is the best person to call. You call someone to pick you up and take you to the meeting, leaving instructions for the auto repair shop to tow the broken-down car and repair it.

All very efficient—and an appropriate use of adrenaline arousal. High adrenaline has helped sharpen your wits, enabling you to make quick decisions and take decisive action. But then you get to your meeting and discover that your heart is pounding, your hands are cold (everyone you shake hands with remarks about it), and there is a slight tremble in your fingers. You can't think very clearly because your mind is on your broken-down car. You're still in high gear. Is this helpful? No, it isn't.

The emergency is past, but a vague fear keeps you on edge. Force of habit keeps your adrenaline pumping, even though you're coasting downhill. This is the time to go into a relaxed state to quickly restore your system to normal operation again.

BRING DOWN YOUR ADRENALINE LEVEL

Adrenaline surges should not be allowed to continue beyond the immediate legitimate emergency that provokes them. As soon as possible after the emergency, you should bring down your level of arousal. To let it continue in high gear or, for that matter, fail to be aware that the adrenaline emergency has ended, is to court disaster in the form of stress damage. You must move back to a non-emergency mode as quickly as possible.

I realize that this may sound easier than it really is to put into practice, and if you do not know how to relax your body and your mind, it certainly will be difficult. The relaxation exercises described in chapter 12 should be practiced ahead of time as a way of "inoculating" yourself for the times you will need them. Preparing yourself for these emergencies ahead of time will assure your success. The marathon athlete does not wait until just before the race to prepare for the challenging and grueling demand ahead. The airline pilot does not wait until an emergency to practice what he will do in the event of an engine problem. Weeks or months of practice, fitness training, or rehearsal of emergency procedures will precede the race or flying crisis. You cannot hope to be effective in adrenaline management unless you master the basic techniques of relaxation ahead of time.

HOW CAN ADRENALINE LEVELS BE LOWERED?

Once you have decided you don't need the adrenaline you are recruiting (or once the emergency is over), it's important to bring your adrenaline down as rapidly as possible.

If you can, it helps to excuse yourself and find somewhere to be by yourself for a few minutes. But if you can't, don't despair. You can just as effectively bring your adrenaline under control on a crowded train, in a busy shopping mall, at an intense board meeting, or during a final examination, as you can in the quietness of your own bedroom.

Each of us will need to find the specific adrenaline reducing tactics that work best for us. For many, there will be some form of *self-talk*. Some people will merely need to say to themselves, *Now calm yourself. Life is not a hundred-yard dash. You must disengage from this conflict; it's not important that you win.* Others will need to be tougher on themselves.

Find your own strategy of self-talk (some ideas are listed below) and tailor it to your personality. Be tough or tender—just convince yourself that you must get your adrenaline down.

The primary and most successful method for adrenaline reduction is conscious physical relaxation. When you relax the body, the mind can't keep itself in a state of emergency. A relaxed body begins to relax the mind.

Exercises for learning relaxation are described in chapter 12. Once you have learned them, you can do them almost anywhere and at anytime.

In addition to relaxation, you should also do some mild exercise. If you are seated, get up and take a stretch. Walk around the table or down the corridor. Look through a window at the clouds outside. This will help distract your mind. If you can, go outside. Feel the sun and smell the flowers. Pick a leaf and note its intricacy and wonder. All the time, consciously relax your muscles. A combination of healthy, positive self-talk and physical relaxation can effectively lower adrenaline in most circumstances. Try the following when you can't lower it to a comfortable level:

1. *Remind yourself that you are just a very tiny cog in a very big cosmos.* Stop playing Messiah and you will have considerably less stress! *Remember that if you have been or are going to be successful, it will probably not be because of your Type-A behavior.* Society does reward you for your hurriedness, but real happiness and long-term success only come from living a balanced life.

2. *If you feel you must succeed in the situation before you, ask yourself: Is the price I am going to pay for this really worth the benefit?* The answer will probably help restore a sense of perspective and remind you of your long-term goals and values.

3. *Force yourself to deliberately slow down.* Develop the ability to slow down when you need to. Ask yourself: *What's the real hurry?* The sun won't come up before tomorrow morning, no matter how much you rush. Few friends, coworkers, or

superiors will have any more respect for you because you "hurry" yourself, than if you pace yourself. If anything, most would trust you more if you slowed down a little.

4. *Quickly resolve those emotions that are adrenaline "biggies"*— anger, resentment, frustration, irritation, and over excitement. Apologize if you are wrong. Bury the hurts that are due to your oversensitivity, and forgive those hurts that are due to others' insensitivity or cruelty. (Later in this chapter, you will find some tips on how to do this.) *Review your life goals.* Ask, *Is the challenge before me absolutely necessary to my life goal?* Consider whether you would want this goal to be destroyed in your quest for success. Consider whether your goals need to change.

5. *Look closely at the faces of those around you.* What do they tell you? You can learn a lot from how others are killing themselves. Looking at their faces can also show you what you are missing. Do they seem like friends or foes? Are you forgetting that they are people also, with rights, longings, aspirations, and a need for love? Do them and yourself a favor by easing up on your demands on them.

6. *Relax your expectations and try to really enjoy the world around you.* Recover your total personality and poise. Try to be gracious and keep a clear perspective about what is *really important and necessary.*

Why don't you, right at this moment, go find a bird to watch! Surely there are a few in your neighborhood. If you don't have birds near your apartment or office, go to the nearest park.

There's a beautiful story in the Bible about looking at birds. You will find it in Matthew 6:25, 26, and 28:

> "So my counsel is this: Don't worry about *things*—food, drink, and clothes. . . . Look at the *birds!* They don't worry about what to eat . . . And why worry about your clothes? Look at the *field lilies!* They don't worry about theirs." (Living Bible)

In fact, I am going to take a break right now and do just that! I think it will help me reduce the adrenaline I feel rising in my blood, just writing about adrenaline and stress!

PLANNING FOR RECOVERY TIME

We cannot avoid all arousal, all the time, nor should we even try. It is inevitable that there will be periods when our adrenaline is surging strongly and, rather than coming down, it must stay up. When the task is important enough, we need all the energizing and enlivening we can muster!

Perhaps it's when a sick child needs constant attention over many days. Perhaps it's when we've planned a visit to our childhood haunts and find ourselves on a "temporary" high, reliving early life experiences. This happened to me a year ago when I visited my childhood neighborhood in South Africa. I was on an adrenaline high for days! Perhaps it's when we have to complete a research project or host a special dinner party. Or perhaps it's when a friend or family member is in trouble with the law or has a terminal illness. Whatever the task demanding arousal, we have no choice but to give it all we've got until our purpose is accomplished.

What should we do in times like these? It is crucial to *plan adequate time for recovery.* Sooner or later the crisis will be over, and that is when you must make time for adequate recuperation of your adrenaline system. It is simply a matter of responsible self-management.

I used to be the world's worst when it came to allowing adequate recovery time. As I mentioned in an earlier chapter, I am sometimes asked to speak at retreats or deliver a series of lectures away from home. In the past, I would leave my office around midday on a Friday, fly to the East Coast, speak at a meeting that evening, present three seminars on Saturday, preach at two services on Sunday morning, and fly back to Los Angeles that afternoon, arriving home a little before bedtime. And the next morning I would be up at six-thirty and at my office for my first appointment at eight!

What's wrong with this schedule? For one thing, I had high blood pressure. For another, life seemed less than satisfying. Such nonstop, rush-about activity without adequate time for recovery eventually resulted in increased wear and tear on the body, elevated cholesterol, and adrenaline exhaustion—not to mention possible heart disease.

No matter how I try to relax while I am on a trip, my system stays aroused. I sleep in a strange bed (which often reduces sleep effectiveness), meet new people (which creates a certain amount of anxiety), and fulfill a demanding speaking schedule (which keeps my adrenaline pumping at a high rate for the whole time). When I come home my body simply needs time to crash, recover, and revitalize itself. And I must allow time for this also!

Fortunately, my eyes were opened before I did too much damage. I realized what I was doing to myself. That is when I became determined to always *plan on recovery time*. Now, whenever my schedule threatens to become especially demanding, I plan ahead for recovery afterwards. For instance, if I have a long series of speaking engagements, I clear my schedule for a day or two afterwards so there is time for rest. AND I DON'T FEEL GUILTY FOR DOING THIS!

Sometimes it may only mean sleeping in a few extra hours the next morning and going to my office around noon. Sometimes it means taking a day or two to compensate for the lack of a "Sabbath" rest. Sometimes it simply means that I schedule a day of "lighter" work. The specifics are not important, but the principle is!

PREPARING FOR TIMES OF STRESS

Another way I plan ahead for times of extra stress is by trying to keep change at a minimum. For instance, I keep my travel time as short as possible and seldom plan two speaking engagements to follow one after the other, no matter how "efficient" it may seem to speak back-to-back. It is easy to overlook just how stressful change *is*. Just being away from home, staying in strange places, and meeting new people can be enough "change" to cause me overstress. So in times of extra stress, it helps to *keep other change at a minimum*.

Still other ways I prepare for a demanding schedule are:

- sleeping a little extra ahead of time
- cutting back on extraneous activities
- making sure I do my relaxation exercises faithfully
- planning all my activities as efficiently as I can
- restricting the demands I allow others to impose on me.

This last suggestion takes a lot of assertiveness to implement but is very important, especially in times of extra demand. We have to be firm with those who would clutter up our lives with trivia. We must be clear about our own priorities so we can make good decisions about what we will and will not do. And we must free ourselves of excessive guilt about not doing what everyone wants us to do. As we get older, and by that I mean past thirty, we must become more determined to limit the unnecessary use of adrenaline by managing the circumstances that create it.

AVOIDING THE ADRENALINE EMOTIONS

Emotions serve many different purposes in our lives. Some are designed to provide healing. Surprisingly, *depression* is one of the healing emotions. It removes us temporarily from our environment so that our bodies and minds can be restored.

Other emotions are "warning signals." They tell us something is happening to us—especially when something is wrong. Anxiety and guilt fall in this category. So also do the emotions I call the "adrenaline emotions," because they tend to stimulate adrenaline production. Included here would be:

- anger
- frustration
- irritation
- resentment
- hostility

These emotions, if not attended to, can send us to an early grave because of the stress they cause. Most of us know people, if we are not that way ourselves, who get angry whenever they are disappointed. Their frustration tolerance is extremely low. Whenever they can't get their way they explode, hold grudges, and carry resentment fed by impeccable memories . . . forever. And, unfortunately, our culture glorifies these emotions!

Actually, the last three of the adrenaline-producing emotions mentioned above are closely related to the first one—anger. Simply speaking, anger in all its forms is bad for us! Why? Because it triggers the "fight or flight" reaction more easily and strongly than any other emotion, and can keep it going longer.

In its early stages, anger is simply a signal alerting us to a violation of our rights. The feeling of anger is the "pain" of our psychological disposition. It tells us that we have been transgressed. At this point, there is nothing wrong with anger; in fact, it is healthy. But from this point, two things can go wrong:

1. We don't pay attention to the anger.
2. Anger, the *feeling* is translated into anger, the *behavior*— such as aggression and hostility.

The ultimate purpose of anger is to prepare us to fight. (It is the "fight" part of the "fight or flight" response). Anger creates in us a powerful need for revenge. And therein lies its greatest danger, both to ourselves and others. All spouse abuse, family violence, and many murders owe their origins to this very primitive response.

But I am really not concerned here about the effect of anger on others or in society as a whole, important as this effect may be. What I want to emphasize is *how destructive anger can be to the one who is angry.*

Being angry for any length of time almost certainly increases the level of adrenaline. It raises the blood pressure, causes hand temperature to drop, and disrupts the digestive process. The reason is simple: The body, fed by ideas from the mind, is kept in a constant state of *readiness to fight.* Thus, the heightened and persistent level of chronic hostility, like any form of continuous overstress, will cause accelerated deterioration of the cardiovascular system and a host of other stress symptoms such as headaches, ulcers, and stomach problems. This is why the characteristic of hostility in the Type-A personality has been identified as the most critical of all.

Anger—with its cohorts of resentment, hostility, frustration, and irritability—will also be *loaded with fear*. We are afraid of those who hurt us, and the more afraid we become, the more we will tend to harbor grudges and keep our resentment alive. For legal as well as moral reasons, we can never repay those who hurt us, so we are left to suffer the consequences of our anger *within ourselves*. Those who hurt us then cause us *double damage*—the original hurt, compounded by the damage our own anger does to ourselves.

This truth came home to me forcibly some years ago when I was on a speaking tour in Australia and decided I would learn how to throw a boomerang. Early one sunny morning during a break, I enrolled in "boomerang school" at a nearby park. The instructor showed me how to stand, hold the boomerang, and throw it. I did exactly as I had been instructed: That little piece of twisted wood left my hand like a bullet, twirling furiously as it described a wide circle. Then, as I stood staring in awe, it came back toward me. Now, I knew that was the whole point of the exercise, but I was nevertheless taken by surprise!

My instructor shouted, "Duck!" Luckily I obeyed, or I would have been seriously injured. That sucker passed over me right where my head had been . . . spinning furiously! Boomerangs are dangerous weapons!

But so is anger. *It injures the one who throws it about.*

I believe this so very strongly that I have tried with my utmost ability to literally follow the admonition: "Let not the sun go down upon your wrath" (Eph. 4:26). Modern stress psychologists would heartily agree with this ancient advice. The sooner we bring our anger under control by addressing ourselves to its source, the better.

The following may help you to reduce your anger proneness:

1. *Make sure you include non-angry people among your closest friends.* Angry people fuel each other. If you are easily influenced by them, avoid them. Chronically hostile people don't make good friends anyway; their anger is too contagious.

2. *Accent the flaws in your own personality.* If you are unduly sensitive to criticism, learn how to respond more constructively. If you keep expecting others to be perfect (usually because you fear your own imperfections), consciously grant them the privilege of "imperfection." Work at accepting them *as they are*, not as you would like them to be.

3. *Stop believing that anger is good for you.* It isn't. The "good" feeling you get when you are angry is nothing more than an adrenaline rush.

4. *Try to be more assertive with people who hurt you.* Tell them the truth—that their actions are painful and that they violate your rights. If they won't listen and back off, avoid them. We are called to "love" each other, but this doesn't mean we must place ourselves where we can be continually offended or punished. It's easier, and more constructive, to love some people from a distance!

5. *Stop being critical of others.* Remember that the most common reason we find other people obnoxious is that *they reflect our own weaknesses.* Angry people see anger in others because they subconsciously recognize their own personality flaws. So work at seeing the good in others—perhaps you'll begin to become a little more like them!

6. *If there are life circumstances* that are causing you ongoing hostility, find someone to talk with about it. A brief period of psychotherapy might help you come to understand the reason for your hostility. Perhaps you need the courage to move on to a new job or change your circumstances in some other productive way. Life is too short and too precious to be wasted on trying to make a good thing out of impossible circumstances. Talking with someone else might help you see a way out.

HOW TO COPE WITH THE STRESS OF PAIN

In chapter 8, I showed how pain can be an unrecognized source of stress. When we are in pain, our bodies react as to danger, and adrenaline surges.

Like anger, pain has a legitimate function; it alerts us that something has gone wrong. But after that initial purpose has been served, it can simply linger as a source of stress. For people suffering from certain disorders such as arthritis, skeletal misalignments, and cancer, pain can be a constant and stressful part of life. To help cut down on the stress of pain, the following suggestions may be helpful:

1. *Try not to dwell on it.* Pain, like many other sensations, is enhanced by how much attention we focus on it. Athletes who are hurt while playing have been known to be unaware of their pain until afterwards. This is due in part to high adrenaline, but it is also because the athletes get caught up with *distracting activity.* When we are immersed in an activity or are diverted by interesting conversation or hobbies, pain is easier to tolerate. So if you are experiencing long-term pain, avoid boredom, inactivity, or just plain brooding. This will not make the pain go away, but it will cut down on the stress pain causes.

2. *Try to avoid becoming anxious.* Anxiety makes pain worse. I prove this in an experiment I conduct every time I go to the dentist. If I don't worry, I feel less pain. I've proven this many times. If I fidget, become tense, and exaggerate my impending doom, I ache more—every prick of the needle hurts.

3. *Relax between your periods of business.* Why is relaxation so important to pain management? We have within our bodies a very effective pain inhibition system. It is biochemical in nature and is the body's own powerful painkiller—the *endorphins* I described in an earlier chapter.

Certain natural experiences help to increase endorphins, so the more we engage in them, the more we limit our pain. For example, in the last stage of pregnancy the amount of painkiller in the mother's brain rises quite markedly in order to help prepare her for the pain of childbirth. Also, during certain types of stress—the good kind—high adrenaline helps mask pain.

Now, I'm not suggesting we all go out and get pregnant or divvy up some good stress. I mention these merely to show that the body *can* produce more natural painkillers. Relaxation itself can do it, and it is easier and cheaper. Relaxation creates a state of low arousal in which the body produces more endorphins. The more we relax, the more we protect ourselves from pain. So learning how to achieve deep relaxation and practicing it often can dramatically reduce the amount of stress that comes from being in pain.

MEDICATION FOR OVERACTIVE ADRENAL SYSTEMS

There are those whose adrenal systems are overly reactive. We call them "hot reactors." The slightest demand raises their adrenaline excessively. Their systems become hypersensitive and overly active, so blood pressure soars, the heartbeat becomes erratic, and a feeling of panic can easily set in. Sometimes this sensitivity is brought on by prolonged stress. Sometimes it is due to genetic factors or even disease.

Fortunately, effective medical treatment is available for this condition. Medication can control adrenaline production very effectively. While I do not advocate the excessive use of these drugs because they can tend to make our bodies "lazy" and include some unfortunate side-effects at higher doses, such as impotence, there are situations when their use is appropriate.

If you are prone to panic attacks, have high blood pressure or erratic heartbeats, medication to control adrenaline may be needed. See your physician, who must prescribe it, as soon as possible. It may also be necessary to add a tranquilizer, because the natural tranquilizers in the brain have been depleted by high or prolonged stress. A physician will know how to treat this condition or will refer you to a specialist. The treatment is most effective, so don't delay in getting this kind of help if it is called for.

The Secret of Sleep

Tonight millions of Americans will crawl into bed, draw up the covers, snuggle onto soft pillows, and try to go to sleep—without much success. They will toss and turn for a long time before finally slumbering off to dreamland. One estimate is that as many as fifty million Americans sleep poorly, if at all. For most, their sleeplessness will be caused by hyper-arousal—they will be "high" on too much adrenaline.

Not only will they sleep poorly, but many will rationalize and make excuses about their sleeplessness, believing that they sleep too much anyway. I wonder who started this erroneous idea? More suffering and discomfort is caused by this faulty idea than I care to enumerate. The truth is that *we need all the sleep we can get* if we are going to avoid stress disease. Sleep is an important antidote for the stress of everyday living, and those who sleep better are *less damaged* by their stress. I would even go so far as to say that too much sleep is almost never a problem for healthy people. Your body wakes you up whenever it has had enough rest. Sounds revolutionary, doesn't it? But these are very carefully considered convictions on my part—so read on.

It is true that some people may use excessive sleep as a form of escape. When they are depressed or worried they stay under the covers and avoid life. But this is a symptom of some deep-seated disturbance and an unhealthy way of coping with life. That is not what I am advocating here.

There are also some rare illnesses in which the brain keeps wanting to go to sleep. One of them is called "narcolepsy," a disorder in which a sudden urge to sleep overtakes the sufferer, usually during emotional excitement. All the muscles become paralyzed, and the sufferer cannot resist the sudden onset of sleep. Another is "sleeping sickness," a disease caused by a bite from an infected tsetse fly which is usually found in Africa or South America.

But again, these are diseases—not normal states. For most of us, sleep is an important restorative and relaxing state of the mind and body, and we need as much of it as we can possibly get. We neither abuse it nor do we use it for unhealthy reasons. Despite this, we've been deluded into thinking that we sleep too much, a significant factor in predisposing our culture to high risk for stress disease.

A good night's sleep, one that is restful and calm, should be high on our list of priorities. It is important for preventing and fighting disease (an important link with the immune system has already been shown), lowering anxiety, and avoiding stress-induced heart disease.

SOME DISASTROUS MISINFORMATION

Many aspects of sleep remain a mystery. Some people have even wondered if sleep was necessary at all. I wonder what sort of world they've been living in! If nothing else, too little sleep leads to irritability and fatigue.

One source for the idea that we sleep too much probably comes from research carried out in the early fifties. An insurance company wanted to know the effect of sleep on longevity, so they surveyed hospital patients and discovered that the longer someone slept, the shorter their life expectancy.

For many years afterwards, the popular belief was that if you slept too much, you shortened your life. I remember reading about this in my early adulthood and deliberately trying to shorten my sleep time—with disastrous results.

What eventually came to light was that the hospital study was bad research. The investigators didn't consider the fact that hospitals tend to have a large number of terminally ill people anyway. And it is certainly true that when you are very sick, you sleep a lot more. Their statistics were slanted by erroneous assumptions made from observations of the sleeping patterns of people who were already at the end of their lives!

This research has long since been debunked, yet many still believe we'll live shorter lives if we sleep longer or we'll live longer if we sleep less. The truth of the matter is, we do not get enough sleep. Most adults are chronically tired or sleepy because they don't go to bed at a reasonable hour.

Evidence for this was brought to light by the National Commission on Sleep Disorders established by Congress. The commission heard from 235 sleep experts and published its findings in January 1993.[1]

Among its many findings, the commission learned that a substantial number of Americans are functionally handicapped by sleep deprivation on any given day. Furthermore, one in five suffers from "stress-related insomnia." I could have told them that! Whenever a person goes to bed with his mind racing with uncompleted work or a sense that he's goofed, or if the mind is not at peace, the person will sleep less than the body actually needs!

A lack of sufficient sleep does not only produce more stress, but it also makes one less able to think clearly and creatively. Work efficiency goes down, more mistakes are made, and stress levels soar even higher. Most important of all, the adrenaline level is too high and altogether, this makes for a very bad package of stress producers.

Effective stress management requires that we learn how to sleep better and longer, and my purpose is to help you improve your sleep habits so as to improve your resistance to stress.

It is true that sleep needs vary among individuals and at different stages of life. These variations are, in my opinion, not as great as we have been led to believe and reflect variations in habit and levels of arousal as much as they do biological rhythms. Some people condition themselves to behave as "night" people, while others consistently reinforce fewer sleeping hours. These variations seem to be more psychological than physiological.

WHAT CAUSES SLEEPLESSNESS?

There are many reasons why a person doesn't get a good night's sleep. These include poor sleep habits such as going to bed too late or at irregular hours, unfamiliar surroundings, too much anxiety, debilitation, depression, overuse of caffeine, or the abuse of drugs and alcohol.

However, one very simple, commonly overlooked factor contributing to sleeplessness is elevated adrenaline. If you are excited, charged, energized, challenged, anxious, or worried, your adrenaline goes up—and sleep goes out the window. Your adrenaline is designed to make you less sleepy—but only in response to emergencies.

It is here that we see a connection between the incidence of heart disease and poor sleeping habits. I am currently conducting a research project that is looking at the sleeping habits of heart-disease victims. Since excessive production of adrenaline is the major cause of heart disease, and since elevated adrenaline also inhibits sleep, there must be a connection between premature heart disease and a reduced need for sleep. If we can establish that those who sleep poorly or insufficiently are at greatest risk for heart disease, we may have a powerful diagnostic pointer for cardiovascular disease. More importantly, it is just possible that helping someone sleep longer will help to bring down adrenaline and prevent heart disease.

It is not clear which comes first in this chicken-and-egg situation. Is it the lowered adrenaline that increases sleep and protects the heart, or is it the extra sleep that lowers the adrenaline? Actually, it doesn't really matter which comes first—as long as we achieve the desired end result.

The heart-disease sufferers I have studied to date have all confirmed my suspicion; almost all have had poor sleeping habits. It goes with being a Type-A personality. They don't sleep enough; they sleep very lightly; they can't get to sleep easily; or, if they do sleep, they wake up early and then can't get back to sleep again.

Why? Their minds are very active and they are too excited or fearful most of the time. Their minds won't give the adrenal system any peace. Instead of sleeping, they use the nighttime to finish projects, think up new challenges, fight their battles out in fantasy, or worry about the next day. I know—I'm as guilty as anyone!

Not surprisingly, many of these high-risk individuals find it quite easy to sleep during the daytime, or on a couch in front of the television. The moment they go to bed they are wide awake.

HOW MUCH SLEEP DO WE NEED?

This is the million-dollar question, and I know I am going to ruffle quite a few feathers with my answer! If you believe you only need five hours of sleep, chances are you'll only sleep five hours. Our behavior tends to be consistent with our beliefs—that's a psychological fact! To sleep longer, you must be convinced that you need more sleep—so let me try some persuasive reasoning.

There is emerging among sleep experts more definitive answers to the question of how much sleep we need—and it's more than we're getting. The National Commission on Sleep Disorders recommends that the average person get a minimum of seven to eight hours of sleep. I believe this is on the low end, as I will demonstrate.

When I am faced with an unpleasant or novel demand on a certain day, I tend to wake up (or rather be awakened by my adrenaline) earlier than usual and do not sleep as much the night before. It's as if my body knows I have an extra demand or challenge facing me, so it provides me with extra energy in preparation, but at the expense of my sleep. This is no problem if it only occurs infrequently.

Whenever I have a period of extra work or am facing deadlines that must be met, my need for sleep also diminishes. My mind tells my sleep control center that I can cope with less "lullaby." But—and here is the rub—I pay for lack of sleep later with an accumulated deficit! As long as my adrenaline is up, I'm fine and don't feel the need for the sleep. My adrenaline keeps me awake by providing extra energy but also reduces my reserves. When it finally lets up, I crash—and I will pay for this abuse with more fatigue than usual, even becoming depressed from the exhaustion. At this point, I will require extra sleep to compensate for the overuse. The reduced need for sleep produced by my elevated adrenaline is only a temporary state, not intended for everyday living.

How can so many people sleep for so few hours and still believe they are doing well? I think it is because they are operating on too much adrenaline. People who sleep little have functioned this way for so long that it has become a way of life. Their systems are adapted to high arousal, and they seldom relax enough to achieve an adequate period of sleep.

This is where I believe those sleep researchers who have tried to determine what our normal sleep needs are have missed the mark. In trying to find out how much sleep we really need, they have surveyed large numbers of urban adults, asking, "How many hours do you sleep?" The information they arrive at with this approach merely tells us how *common* a certain amount of sleep is. Usually, it is between five and seven hours a night, with most people sleeping six or seven hours.

This type of survey research can be misleading because the majority of the people in our urban society are Type A's—highly driven, highly stressed, and performance-oriented. They suffer from too much adrenaline arousal as a matter of course, so how can their sleep needs be labeled as "normal"?

We need research that will look at healthy, low-stressed people and determine how much sleep they get in order to remain healthy. This data will probably give us different norms. My prediction, based on years of clinical experience, is that it will be higher than the seven to eight hours recommended by the Commission on Sleep, and more like eight to nine hours per night. Who knows—it might even be ten! My wife will be pleased to hear this.

It is my belief that for good stress-disease prevention, you should aim to get between eight and ten hours of sleep each night (an average of nine), with some going as high as eleven hours. There are some individual differences such as age, lifestyle, and physical health that will cause the actual amount needed to vary, but an average of nine hours seems to offer the best protection and leaves a little to spare for emergencies. Under conditions of high stress, the *apparent* need for sleep diminishes and extra sleep should be provided as soon as the stress period is over. If the stress demand continues, extra "rest" time should be added during the day.

The Commission on Sleep introduced a novel but accurate way of thinking about sleep. Our actual sleep needs may be likened to a bank account—the commission calls it the "sleep bank." We make deposits when we sleep sufficiently, withdrawals when we don't. Not getting enough sleep is like being overdrawn at the sleep bank! If we are too much overdrawn, our risk for stress disease goes up. To get it down, we must keep our sleep accounts current. We must make extra deposits when we know our sleep will be disturbed and after stress periods. Catching that Saturday afternoon nap may be healthier than we think!

I am convinced that most of us could improve our physical and emotional health dramatically if we just slept or rested a little longer than usual.

ORDINARY INSOMNIACS

One in four adults has insomnia, according to the Sleep Research Center at Stanford University. They have trouble either falling asleep or staying asleep. They approach bedtime with a high state of dread, and pray for the night to pass quickly. Some experience this discomfort only occasionally, while for others it is a chronic problem. Chronic sufferers depend almost entirely on sleeping pills for what little rest they get.

My purpose here is not to focus on the problem of persistent insomnia (which calls for professional help), but on the more common problem of periodic insufficient sleep, whether self-induced or without choice.

We all experience temporary bouts of insomnia. It happens in the healthiest of people, but strikes most often when we are overstressed. Seldom does it happen when we are on vacation— unless our idea of a vacation is mountain-climbing in Tibet!

Many people don't believe they should sleep very much, so they wake themselves up with alarm clocks or deliberately stay up late, working or watching TV. They may label themselves as "night people"—except they get up early too. Other "night people" prefer to work late and then sleep into the day. They usually suffer from not getting enough sleep.

Most of those who sleep little relish their reduced need for sleep and believe themselves to be more efficient and productive. In many cases, this is simply not true. But even if they are right, there is still a price to pay for this "efficiency." It is the same price they pay for using a small motor to do a big motor's job—*burnout*. The human body is like a motor. It can become overheated and overused if it doesn't have enough rest. And while it may seem to be working efficiently, it is wearing out before it should.

WHAT HAPPENS WHEN WE SLEEP

The precise function of sleep remains a mystery, despite all our research. We know what it does in general terms, but no one really knows what happens when we sleep . . . or even why sleep is necessary. Why not just spend nine hours resting? Why sleep?

Research on prolonged sleep deprivation—during which people are kept awake for many days—hasn't helped solve the mystery. In fact, it has been quite misleading because artificially induced sleep deprivation cannot be equated with the reduced need for sleep due to adrenaline arousal. The one stimulus is from without, the other from within—and this makes all the difference in the effect on the human body.

What happens when we sleep? After about fifteen to thirty minutes of relaxation, the prospective sleeper reaches a stage of semiconsciousness which is neither waking nor sleeping. One may think he is still awake because he can think and hear noises, but he is nevertheless in a state of early sleep.

After a few more minutes, the sleeper suddenly falls into unconsciousness. This final shift from drowsiness to sleep only takes a second or two—but no one is awake to explain how it happens! As the sleeper moves from a state of semi-awareness to deep sleep, the brain's electrical waves become slower and slower until finally, after about ninety minutes, dreaming becomes possible. Then the body jerks mildly and the eyelids flutter.

The various transformations brought about by sleep are quite obvious. We breathe more slowly. Our eyeballs turn up and out, our fingers grow cold, and our toes warm. Blood pressure falls rapidly and is lowest about three hours after the onset of sleep. We change positions from twenty to sixty times during the night without knowing it, and for a few moments every ninety minutes or so we may return to semiconsciousness for a brief while. Then slowly (unless something like an alarm clock disturbs the process) our sleep becomes lighter. Consciousness flickers, fails again, flickers—and then we are awake. Another day has dawned!

Perhaps we'll yawn a few times to inhale extra oxygen and lower the carbon dioxide accumulated in the body as a result of muscular inactivity. We may still feel tired, especially if our adrenaline is low, but this isn't necessarily a bad sign. To wake up tired, if we have slept long, can be good news if we are fighting stress disease. It means our bodies have really switched off. After three or four nights of deep, long sleep, the feeling of tiredness on waking passes off, and we awake refreshed and replenished in body and spirit.

TYPES OF SLEEP

There are two basic types of sleep: *dream sleep* and *non-dream sleep*. They are also known as *"REM" sleep* and *"NREM" sleep*. The acronym "REM" simply stands for "rapid eye movement," because it has been found that during dream sleep, the eyelids make rapid jerking movements while the eyeballs move around. "NREM" simply means "non-REM," or non-dreaming sleep.

What functions do REM and NREM sleep serve? NREM, or non-dreaming sleep, is a lighter stage that seems to be important for biochemical restoration of the brain and for physical rest. If you do heavy manual labor, you need more non-dream sleep. REM, or dreaming sleep, is the deepest stage and is important for the consolidation of memory and learning, as well as for sorting and storing information in the brain. About 25 percent of our sleep should be the REM type, and the remainder should be NREM. If you work with your mind, you will need more dream sleep. The lighter NREM sleep is important to REM sleep, because it is only after a certain amount of NREM sleep that you may pass into REM sleep. Without adequate NREM sleep, dreaming can't occur.

When we first go to sleep, we are in non-dream sleep. Then about every ninety minutes or so, we pass into dream sleep and stay there for a few minutes. After dreaming for awhile (whether or not we remember our dreams), we may return to very light sleep or even wakefulness.

Since light, NREM sleep is so important, and since we often think we are awake when we are, in fact, semiconscious, it is important not to force ourselves into full wakefulness during these periods of non-dreaming sleep. Many people will get out of bed, go to the bathroom, eat a snack, or watch TV—thinking they can't sleep anyway, so why not do something—when they are actually in a light sleep state. Getting up usually brings them to a state of real wakefulness, and then it is difficult to get back to deep sleep. If instead of getting up, they would just lie still and relax, realizing that they are still experiencing an important part of the sleep cycle, they would soon drift back into a deep sleep again. One can spend several hours in a light doze and still wake up feeling refreshed!

This dipping in and out of deep sleep is normal—in fact, there is no other way to sleep. We only create sleeping problems when we fail to understand the value of light sleep and semi-wakefulness.

One last word about dream sleep: For people who do mental work, insufficient dream sleep can cause wake-up headaches, apathy, poor judgment, increased sensitivity to pain, and a decrease in alertness. To make sure you get enough dream sleep, you must put in a certain amount of light sleep. So whatever your need, physical rest or mental rest, sleeping for a long enough period of time is essential for good health.

DETERMINING HOW MUCH SLEEP YOU NEED

Whether or not you are a "night" person, and whether you think you sleep too little or too much, the first step toward developing a healthy sleep pattern is to determine how much sleep *you* need to function at your best. Forget about everyone else—you may just be different!

There are two ways to determine how much sleep you need. The first way is to begin by adding sleep in half-hour increments to your existing sleep period by going to bed earlier or waking up later. But give yourself time to adjust to each change. Add the first half-hour, then keep this up for five to seven days. Observe what happens to your emotions, creative thinking, and energy level.

The reason you must let the extra sleep "settle down" for a few days into a pattern is that if you are trying to lower your adrenaline at the same time, you may initially feel more tired than usual upon waking. This is a good sign—your system is really winding down. Welcome it! By the fifth or sixth day, the benefits of the extra sleep will be obvious. Then add a further half-hour of sleep and keep this schedule for five to seven days to observe the results.

Sooner or later, you will reach the point of no further improvement, and it will be easy to decide how much sleep makes you feel alive and most able to function at your best. For most of us, it can be between one and two hours more sleep than we are presently getting.

The second way to find your optimal sleep period is to recall your last extended vacation and try to remember how much sleep you got during the second week of that vacation. If it was a "real" vacation, it probably went like my last one in Hawaii. As I related earlier, for the first four or five days I was restless. I kept waking up early, still feeling tired. I fidgeted, couldn't sit still for very long, and kept wanting to "do something." I was experiencing "adrenaline withdrawal" because my body wasn't used to the reduced demands of vacation life.

But slowly I settled down and my sleep improved. By the end of the week, I could get to sleep easily and slept about one-and-a-half hours longer than usual. I believe this longer sleep period is what is best for me—if only I could achieve it during normal work time as well! I compromised by adding an extra forty-five minutes to my sleep cycle and feel much better because of it.

RULES FOR BETTER SLEEP

Since the quality of sleep is as important as its duration, attention should be given to every aspect of the sleeping environment: A comfortable bed, quiet atmosphere, and adequate time allowed for sleep *are absolute essentials*. Attention to the following simple rules will further improve your sleep:

- *Rule 1:* Go to bed and get up at the same time every day, weekends included. A regular sleep routine builds a healthy habit and conditions the body's natural internal clock.

- *Rule 2:* Do not do any work, read novels, or watch TV late at night if these cause your adrenaline system to become aroused. If you can only fall asleep while reading or watching TV, you've got a problem; you've conditioned your body to a bad habit. Start breaking the habit right away.

- *Rule 3:* As early in the evening as possible, reduce the level of illumination by turning down the lights and providing a darkened environment. Darkness starts the production of an important brain hormone called "melatonin." While its precise function is not understood, it is thought to serve as a messenger to the rest of the body, telling it that darkness has arrived and sleep can be prepared.

- *Rule 4:* Avoid alcohol, caffeine, chocolates, spicy or greasy foods (or large amounts of any food), and in the evening, especially near bedtime—although a glass of milk or a light carbohydrate snack may be helpful. People who drink alcohol or smoke often remain awake in bed a long time afterward. In part, this is because they are more tense and adrenally aroused than others (which is why they need the drink or smoke in the first place—to calm down), but also because of the effects these chemicals have on the body. Even though alcohol is commonly thought to make us sleepy, it actually interferes with sleep patterns.

- *Rule 5:* Do not force sleep on yourself. Falling asleep is as natural as falling off a log if you *first* lower your adrenaline arousal and only do soothing, nonstimulating activities in the late evening. Forcing sleep on ourselves only frustrates us further and causes more adrenaline to be secreted—reducing the likelihood that we'll ever get to sleep.

- *Rule 6:* Find a quiet place to sleep. If you live in a noisy environment, invest in ear plugs. They are easy to get used to (I've used them for many years), and they effectively shut out a lot of noise. We sleep deeper and more peacefully if our brains don't have to block out background noises.

- *Rule 7:* Exercise regularly, but do not engage in competitive or strenuous exercise just before you go to bed. Again, very rigorous exercise only raises adrenaline levels. People who exercise often sleep better because the exercise helps to use up surplus adrenaline, release muscular tension, and ventilate lungs. It also creates a physical fatigue that helps the onset of sleep.

- *Rule 8:* Learn a relaxation technique such as the one described in chapter 12. Combine it with a spiritual exercise or prayer if you like. Deep muscle relaxation will help prepare you for sleep.

- *Rule 9:* Untrouble your mind. Learn the value of forcing your mind away from problems; if you must think, divert your thoughts to less troublesome matters.

- *Rule 10:* If you awaken during the night, don't get up unless you absolutely must. Relax and enjoy your light sleep. Revel in the luxury of just lying there.

THE HAZARDS OF EVENING AND SHIFT WORK

Unfortunately, many people have to work in the evenings, and this can play havoc with their sleep habits. Ministers must attend evening meetings, doctors must work late at the hospital, and clerks, stockers, waitresses, and waiters must work evenings. For them, sleep will be a challenge. Not only does night work temporarily upset the body's internal clock, but it usually takes between two and four hours after the end of the work period for the adrenaline level to drop low enough for sleep to come on.

This means that if you have a committee meeting that lasts until 10:00 P.M., it may be between midnight and 2:00 A.M. before you can fall asleep. If you are one of these nighttime workers, what can you do about it? First of all, you can reduce these demands on your evenings to a minimum. Second, if you must work nights, then adjust your waking up time by adding extra sleep in the morning to compensate for the lost sleep at night. Third, if you work late only occasionally, get to bed earlier the next evening to make up for the sleep loss. Fourth, don't become frustrated if you can't get to sleep at your usual time. Allow for the extra time it takes for your adrenaline to "come down" and avoid further excitement after your work is over. Many get a "second wind" late in the evening, tackle some extra activities, and can't get to sleep until the early hours of the morning. This can be avoided by going to bed earlier in the evening, before the "second wind" has time to kick in, and by avoiding challenging or stimulating activities late at night.

If you cannot avoid doing "swing shift" work, then careful planning can help you prepare for the changeover period. You can start a week or two before time, gradually adjusting sleeping time to conform to the new schedule. Some extra sleep ahead of time can help your body prepare for the initial sleeplessness and fatigue that will follow the change to a new work schedule.

THE DANGERS OF SLEEPING PILLS

Most experts would agree that sleeping pills should be used only for *occasional* sleeplessness. Natural sleep is far better than induced sleep, and dependence on an artificial preparation for proper sleep on a regular basis creates havoc within the body. A conference of experts a few years ago, assembled by the National Institute of Health, warned against using sleeping pills for more than a month at a time. Unfortunately, many millions of people throughout the country depend almost entirely on sleeping preparations for their rest.

Excessive reliance on artificial sleep reduces the body's ability to return to natural sleep. It is better to try to sleep without medication and allow the body to return to its natural ways, even if it means enduring a few nights of sleeplessness, than it is to resort to the use of sleeping pills. While the drugs that help us to sleep are not necessarily harmful in and of themselves, they are habit-forming and make the body "lazy." One never feels really refreshed after a night of artificial sleep.

Depending on the type of sleep medication used, different aspects of normal sleep will be disturbed. Some medications reduce REM sleep and disrupt dreaming, thus disturbing the brain's organizing ability. Others increase REM sleep and reduce NREM. The changes in normal patterns of REM and NREM cut back on emotional restoration, among other things.

Happily, even for the most severe insomniac, rest and a lot of restoration can still take place in the absence of deep sleep. So long as one lies down, immobilizes the body, and receives a measure of relaxation in mind and body, the brain will replenish itself and natural sleep will return in due course. When you can't sleep, don't waste the night worrying about it. Instead, enjoy the quiet and relaxation that rest gives you. Make yourself comfortable and appreciate the privilege of a mind and heart at peace. Contemplate beautiful things, think about hopeful things, and recount the happy times of your life. Each time you do this, your mind will be healing your body and reversing the damage caused by the stress of the day.

I remember a Bible verse my Grandmother would quote at bedtime: "I will both lay me down in peace, and sleep: for thou Lord, only makest me dwell in safety" (Ps. 4:8).

It is still good advice!

- the muscle system

- hand temperature (which represents the degree of blood flow in the hands)

- the mind.

These three systems represent the most important for counteracting the stress response. They are also the easiest to train how to relax. Most of us could benefit beyond anything we could imagine by practicing relaxation of these components of our stress response system on a regular basis.

WHY RELAX?

Relaxation as a treatment modality has been around for thousands of years. Sometimes cloaked as religion, it has been used to produce improved health, often without understanding the essential physiology of the body's use of defenses. The elements often cited are the same that modern relaxation recognizes: a quiet environment, comfortable position, reduced muscle activity, and focused attention.

Until recently, modern medicine has neglected one of the most powerful tools for healing ulcers, headaches, high blood pressure, and stomach problems—simple relaxation. It is only in very recent years that its powerful therapeutic effects have been rediscovered, mainly through a man by the name of Eric Jacobson. He introduced relaxation in 1928 as a treatment for fatigue, debility, nervous disorders, and lowered resistance. He rightly believed that the nervous system cannot be quieted except in conjunction with the muscular system. He developed the technique we now know as *progressive relaxation*, a thoroughly scientific way for producing profound relaxation.

I sincerely believe that if we could all learn effective relaxation of at least one of the major systems of the body, we could put many of the drug companies out of business! We could reduce the demand for tranquilizers, painkillers, and antacids by an unbelievable amount. We would sleep better and live longer.

This is not to deny the very real value of medication. It has its place, and I often refer patients for appropriate prescriptions of these powerful drugs. But the use of drugs by themselves to treat stress—and without counseling to change the underlying cause of overstress—is patent negligence.

If you were to walk down Main Street in your city and stop every person you passed, more than half would tell you they are taking either a painkiller, tranquilizer, or antacid on a regular basis. Modern medicine seems to be almost afraid of allowing us to "heal ourselves" or to let the natural healing power of the body do its own work. Any person who leaves a physician's office without at least one prescription (usually for a tranquilizer) feels as if the doctor hasn't done his or her work. And many physicians are aware of this expectation. Yet almost the same benefit can be achieved through simple relaxation in the many cases where stress is the underlying cause of the problem.

Why relax? Relaxing helps the body and the mind return to their non-aroused states. Relaxing helps us "coast" when we don't need to drive hard or struggle uphill. Most of us try too hard to do the things that should be done easily and automatically. We live with effort instead of ease too much of the time—and this only causes overstress and tension.

Relaxation helps us return to the "easy" way of living. It slows us down to the pace of life at which our body organs can recuperate and prepare us for the next set of challenges.

Relaxation also helps the body to regenerate its energy. Our overdependence on adrenaline, for instance, will eventually lead to fatigue because we burn up too much energy; this impairs our skills and dulls our minds. Restful healing allows the adrenaline system to recover and restore its ability to supply energy in larger quantities when needed. If you want to reduce your distress, YOU MUST RELAX. And you must do it often.

EFFECTS OF RELAXATION ON STRESS-RELATED DISORDERS

There is abundant evidence to prove that effective relaxation reduces symptoms in many disorders, even in those not directly attributable to stress. The bottom line is that relaxation is *good for everything that ails us.* Allow me to highlight a few areas where its efficacy is well-established.

Daily, you should spend at least thirty minutes in deep relaxation. This is such a small part of the day that everyone can afford to do it—and none of us can afford not to. The best time is when you come home from work or when your early evening duties are completed. Parents of small children may find that the best time is right after the children are put to bed. That's when you're likely to need it the most!

Weekly, there should be a longer period of relaxation. Sundays or Sabbaths are ideal. On these days, cut back on work or your regular activities. Take time to put your feet up, have a nap, or *just be lazy.*

Much church activity is, unfortunately, geared to make us even busier on Sundays, and I believe this can be a pitfall. If you are not slowing down significantly on your day of rest, you are going against God's intent, as well as courting stress damage.

Many of us have been raised to feel guilty about being idle for even a few minutes. But for the sake of health—spiritual, emotional, mental, and physical—we must stop our compulsive activity and, if necessary, *force ourselves* into inactivity.

BASIC INGREDIENTS IN ALL RELAXATION

There is nothing mysterious or mystical about relaxation. It is a *natural response of the body* and can be triggered by all of us. In and of itself, it does not have spiritual significance, but as we shall see, it can be combined with prayer and meditation to produce a powerful spiritual exercise. It is something that should become easier as you practice it. Whatever body system you are trying to relax, the following are the basic steps to relaxation:

1. *Sit or lie in a comfortable position.* Pain or pressure will keep you in an aroused state, so try to minimize discomfort. Loosen tight clothing and remove your glasses. Try to provide support for all the undersides of your body.

2. *Ensure you won't be interrupted.* Lock the door; hang out a sign; tell spouse, kids, dogs, and neighbors not to disturb you—or better yet, go where they can't find you. Unplug the phone and make sure the stove is turned off.

3. *Set aside a predetermined amount of time* (say, thirty or forty-five minutes) *for the exercise.* Set an alarm so you won't have to keep checking the time.

4. *Don't fall asleep.* Sleeping is not what relaxation is all about. If you need sleep, go ahead and sleep, but don't confuse sleep with "relaxing." Relaxation is a conscious experience, not a trance or sleep-like state. If you fall asleep when relaxing, you probably need more sleep. It might be a good idea to go back and read chapter 11.

5. *Remain inactive.* Don't fidget, move, get up, or scratch. At first, you'll want to do all this because you will be experiencing withdrawal symptoms from the effect of lowered adrenaline, just as when you stop taking a powerful drug. Just put up with the discomfort and it will pass away. (If the need to scratch becomes unbearable, go ahead and scratch, but return as quickly as possible to the relaxed position.)

6. *Avoid thinking troublesome thoughts.* Set aside your worries. Cast all your worries and cares aside and try to "detach" yourself from your worrisome world for a while and remain free of the demands that press on you.

SPECIFIC RELAXATION TECHNIQUES

I will now describe two more specific relaxation exercises—one for the muscles and one for handwarming. They should first be mastered independently and then tried together if desired. The techniques combine *forced inactivity* with *visual imagery* and *self-talk.* Together, they are quite powerful in producing a deep state of relaxation.

The most effective way to practice these exercises is to read the instructions through once so that you understand them, then record them onto an audio cassette. Play the cassette to yourself as you go through the exercise. In this way, you will become familiar with it and can implement it in other settings by recalling the instructions. And you will not have to interrupt your session by constantly peeking in a book!

If you don't have a cassette recorder, have a friend or family member read the instructions to you or read them over a number of times until you understand what it is you must do.

A Technique for Relaxing Muscles

Make yourself comfortable. Close your eyes and shut out the world. Don't cross your arms or legs. Remove shoes and glasses. Clear your mind of worries or resentments. Claim peacefulness for yourself. Now do the following:

Exercise 1—Stretching. While lying flat on your back, raise your hands above your head and rest them at the back, but don't grasp anything. Take a deep breath. Hold your breath—for a few seconds. Relax and breathe out.

Now, stretch your hands up as far as they will go. Stretch them further. Hold them there. Now push your feet down as far as they will go. Further! Hold your arms and feet stretched out as far apart from each other as possible. Count slowly to 10: 1 . . . 2 . . . 3 . . . 4 . . . 5 . . . 6 . . . 7 . . . 8 . . . 9 . . . 10.

Relax and let your hands and feet return to their original position. Again, repeat the exercise and count: 1 . . . 2 . . . 3 . . . 4 . . . 5 . . . 6 . . . 7 . . . 8 . . . 9 . . . 10.

Repeat the stretching exercise once more.

Breathe in and out slowly and rhythmically for a few minutes. Try to breathe from your abdomen, not your chest. Concentrate on what you are doing. When you breathe in, push your stomach out and down, so that your lower abdomen expands. When you breathe out, pull your stomach in slightly to help your lungs give up their air.

Now remain immobile, resting and relaxing for another twenty or thirty minutes (set a timer before you start).

When your relaxation time is over, get up slowly. Move slowly. Sit up for a short while. Move slowly and peacefully. Then go back to your normal duties, trying to maintain a more restful posture.

When you have mastered the above exercise, try doing it while sitting. Later you'll be able to do it while driving or even working.

TECHNIQUE FOR HANDWARMING

I have already described the importance of handwarming as a way of lowering adrenaline, and explained how to use temperature dots or a thermometer for monitoring your hand temperature. Review again the appropriate section of chapter 9 and make sure you have memorized the temperature values associated with each color reflected by the dot (see Figure 7). If you don't have a thermometer, touch your hand to your face and "feel" the temperature.

Now, put the temperature dot in place on your hand or hold a small thermometer. Note the dot's color or temperature before you start. Even if the temperature dot is a dark blue or violet, the warming exercise can still be beneficial.

Lie on your back, hands at your side, legs uncrossed. Close your eyes. Relax. Drop your lower jaw slightly. Take a deep breath and count to five slowly. Breathe in . . . slowly . . . then exhale, feeling the tension leave your body.

Now concentrate on your hands. What can you feel? A slight tingling? A slight coldness or warmness? Or do you feel numb and detached?

Picture yourself lying in the warm sun. Imagine that you are on a favorite beach, and you can feel the sun beating down pleasurably on your hands. Hold this image. Feel the hands getting warmer. (If you don't care for the sun, make up an image of your own or try rotating through several different images.)

Imagine your hands are immersed in warm water. The warmth comforts and heals your hands. The hands are becoming warmer as you leave them there. Feel the blood vessels of your hand becoming larger. Imagine more and more blood filling your hands. They feel like they are becoming swollen from the life-giving extra blood. They become warmer and warmer.

Say to yourself, "My hands are becoming warmer and warmer. I can feel them getting heavier and heavier." Repeat this over and over until you feel your hands actually getting warmer.

Remain this way for an additional ten to twenty minutes, relaxing and allowing your hands to get warmer and warmer.

When you are finished, note the temperature of your hands on your stress dot or thermometer, or by touching your face. If it shows you are "warmer," you are doing the exercise correctly. If not, try the exercise again later. After some practice, your hands will become noticeably warmer.

Remember, once you have warmed your hands, remain in this warmed condition for a period of time. The benefit comes from *staying warm,* not just becoming warm. You can also try the exercise sitting up.

TRY RELAXING DURING YOUR BUSY DAY

It is important that you take every opportunity you can to consciously *relax!* When you find yourself caught up in a conflict with someone, go aside and relax if possible. When you feel a panic sensation coming over you, try relaxing. If you are worried, tense, or anticipating some troublesome encounter, use relaxation to calm your body . . . and your mind will soon follow.

Don't expect to become good at relaxing overnight, however. Like so many other skills we learn, *relaxation takes practice.* Don't be disappointed if you don't succeed at first, but try and try again. Your very life may depend on it!

When you are relaxing, pay particular attention to the following parts of the body that tend to accumulate tension very easily:

1. *The muscles of the jaw, brow, and forehead.* They need special attention. They tend to show your anxiety and confusion very easily. Consciously relax your brow. Drop your lower jaw. Clenching your teeth is never necessary. Whenever you have a problem to solve, remember to *smooth your brow and drop your jaw.*

2. *Avoid clenching your fists* or holding onto the arm of a chair or your steering wheel. Sometimes tension creates in us a need to "hold onto something." It's as if we fear being thrown off our world. Consciously relax your hands, especially when holding a pen, driving your car, or watching TV.

3. *Relax your stomach muscles.* If you pay attention, you will notice that you often tense your stomach as if to prepare for some blow in the pit of it. Too often, we live on the defensive, constantly prepared for someone to attack us. The brain

receives these protective signals from the stomach and prepares the body for counter-attack. But the attack almost never comes, so why not just relax? Don't always pull your stomach in. Forget about your posture and your figure and occasionally just relax.

4. *Watch how you breathe at all times.* Our breathing shows our stress. There are two methods of breathing—chest breathing and belly (or diaphragm) breathing. Try not to breathe just with your chest muscles. This is nervous breathing, meant only for emergencies. It takes place high in the chest, expanding the rib cage, and it feels shallow. Use your stomach when you breathe.

Try this exercise for improved breathing: Lie on your back and place your left hand on your stomach just below the sternum (breastbone). As you breathe in, make sure you do so by pushing up the stomach. You should *see your hand rise* when you do this. If it doesn't, try pushing it up. As you breathe out, the hand must fall. This is diaphragm breathing. It is relaxing, peaceful—the breathing style of calm people. When you breathe from your belly, you can't remain tense. Always try to breathe this way. It could preserve your life!

Changing Your Type-A Behavior

If you are a Type-B person, you may wish to skip this chapter. On the other hand, you are probably married to a Type-A (or work for one), so why not read it to understand your spouse (or boss) better!

If you are a Type-A person, it is not enough for you to learn how to relax. You must also change your thinking, behavior, and attitudes if you are going to avoid distress and allow an even "wearing out" of all parts of your body.

You can get the most out of every day of your life if you learn to be more balanced in your personality.

But kicking old stress habits isn't easy. It's harder than giving up smoking or learning to squeeze the toothpaste tube from the bottom. Years of the old patterns of thinking and behaving that underlie your Type-A personality are not going to give up the ghost without a fight. Changing will take determination and devotion. But it's crucial to do it now. Don't wait until you are staring at the bright overhead lights of an emergency or operating room with a surgeon about to rearrange the blood vessels of your heart! Do it the "natural" way.

CAN I CHANGE MY PERSONALITY?

Again and again, after teaching a stress management seminar and warning of the dangers of the "hurry sickness" that characterize so many of us, I am asked the question: "Can I really change my personality?"

My first response usually causes a reaction of surprise: "No, you can't change your basic personality." But then I hasten to add the qualifier: "But you *can* change your behavior."

To me, this is wonderful news. It means that if I am a Type-A person—supercharged, super achieving, always in a hurry, impatient, intolerant—I can learn to *behave* like a Type-B person—patient, tolerant, more easygoing. (Actually, you are already aware that I am a Type-A, so I am speaking to myself here as much as to anyone!) If you are a Type-B person, especially if you are at the far end of the continuum where you tend to be a little too slow, never accomplishing much, then you may need to learn how to behave a little more like a Type-A person. So it goes both ways! The whole point is to counterbalance your personality style.

Our behavior—how we react to our environment and its challenges—plays an important part in determining whether and how we experience distress. Many experts believe it is a far more important cause of heart disease than what we eat or inhale or how we exercise our muscles. So changing how we behave in response to stress is vital to our survival.

A report from Stanford University some years ago presented the findings of a three-year study which revealed that heart attack victims who received "Type-A Counseling" had more than 50 percent fewer recurring heart attacks than those who were not counseled. "Type-A Counseling" is simply a way of teaching Type-A people how to behave with less irritation at delays, less anger at hurts, and less aggression at competition. It also teaches them how to relax and enjoy a slower pace of life. It's the sort of thing I am doing here. Without this counseling and encouragement to change their behavior patterns, heart attack victims inevitably go back to creating high levels of adrenaline arousal and merely repeat the disease process all over again. Their "new plumbing" just gets clogged up again!

If it is true that behaving less aggressively can prevent further deterioration of the heart after a first attack, then surely behaving in a more moderate, low-adrenaline manner at an earlier time in life will delay, or perhaps even stop, the decaying of the heart's blood vessels. It is never too late to change. It is also never too *early* to change.

I predicted some years ago that we would see a large increase in rehabilitation and counseling clinics designed to help us overcome our Type-A qualities. The last decade has proven this to be so. Since it is estimated that 75 percent of the large urban population is Type A (about 50 percent in the general population), large numbers of people are affected and afflicted by this personality style.

CHANGING YOUR TYPE-A BEHAVIOR

To be as efficient as I can be in communicating how an individual can change, I want to take you through a series of steps. Be sure to take each step slowly and master it before moving on.

It is characteristic of Type-A people to attempt to take *short-cuts*. But they invariably end up not getting where they want to go because they lose their way. Quick, ready-made solutions are not possible when it comes to changing the deep side of one's personality. Change takes time, effort, and persistence. Type B's have what it takes—but then, the Type-B person doesn't have to change as much about themselves as the Type-A person.

Step 1: Acknowledge Your Type-A Tendencies

It may be a secondary symptom of the disorder itself, or it may just be an aspect of the personality, but Type-A people tend to *deny* the severity of their "hurry sickness." In fact, for every five people who unquestionably exhibit Type-A behavior, perhaps four will underplay the intensity of their problem.

"But I *enjoy* what I am doing," or, "I would *never* get anything done if I were different," are typical excuses. And, unfortunately, our success-driven culture also tends to glorify such dangerous beliefs. As a result, no one wants to admit that he or she has a problem—until the problem gets serious.

I have seen many patients prior to their first heart attack—
Type A's experiencing insomnia or very little sleep, headaches,
tension, anxieties, and the like. They don't stay in therapy; they
play down the relationship between their behavior and their
distress, and consequently they don't change. They don't see
the *need* to change. Some never get a second chance!

So the first step in changing your Type-A behavior is to *admit
your Type-A tendencies.* Be courageous! There is really no stigma
attached, since so many are in the same stress boat with you.
Admitting your destructive behavior simply helps you become
motivated to change.

As reinforcement for your admission, tell someone about it.
Commit to change, and then hold yourself accountable to a friend
or spouse. Accountability will help you work harder at changing
your behavior.

Step 2: Change Your Thinking

Behavior change *begins in the mind.*

I am currently seeing a Type-A man in therapy. He doesn't
object to my telling you his story because he would like others
to get the message.

This man owns his own business and is obsessed with making
money. He thinks about it, fantasizes about it, and dreams about
it all the time. Because he is failing at his goal, he became deeply
depressed some months ago. His was a typical *reactive* depression, a response to a profound sense of loss.

I challenged him to stop thinking about money. "Just think
about work," I suggested. "Dwell on how you love working,
and how you derive satisfaction from seeing a happy customer.
Forget about the by-product of that work, the money you earn.
If you work hard, the money side will take care of itself."

I reminded him that the love of money is the root of all evil.
My words struck home, and he began to change his thinking. As
he *focused on his work* instead of money, his depression soon lifted.
His most recent words to me were, "I've started loving my wife
again. I never expected that to happen just because I stopped
thinking about money!"

Another client said to me, "If I didn't think the way I do, I'd be a happier person." She's right! Our thoughts define us! A lot of our problems are due to the way we think.

There are many helpful books on the market that can help you straighten out your thinking. For my purpose, I want to focus on specific ways *hurried thinking* produces a *hurried personality*.

There are *three ways* that Type-A thinking tends to go wrong:

1. Type A's *think continuously.* Their minds never stop; they think like a concrete mixer—churning, churning, and spewing out a mix of all the ingredients originally put in.

2. Type A's *think rapidly.* Their minds race ahead of their tongues. Other people can't keep pace. Type A's often finish thinking about something before others have even started!

3. Type A's *think polyphasically.* That is, they think on different tracks at the same time. They keep two or three ideas going along simultaneously. It's like thinking in duet, trio, or even in quartet—except there's no harmony, just cacophony. The solution to this type of thinking, then, is to:

   - *Try creating periods of non-thinking.* Make your mind go blank for a while each hour. Focus on some pretty object or peace-inducing verse of poetry. Deliberately choose not to think about but just reflect on it. Stare at it, hold your mind still, and say to yourself, *I will not think—just be.* Do this several times each hour.

   - *Try slowing down your thinking.* Since all thinking is in the form of self-conversation, try speaking to yourself very slowly. This helps to slow down your thinking, just as talking to yourself fast speeds it up. If you speak slowly and deliberately to yourself (and pay attention to what you are saying), you can slow your mind down. Try it now and see how effective it is. Say to yourself, very slowly, *I . . . am . . . not . . . going . . . to . . . think . . . rapidly.* Notice how, during the pauses, you can hold off other thoughts. With practice, your mind will become very calm when you speak this way to yourself.

- *Try thinking* (slowly, of course) *about one thing at a time.* Write your other intruding thoughts on paper to get them out of your mind, just in case you fear forgetting them. Then focus on just one thought at a time. With some practice, this will become quite easy also.

Step 3: Change Your Attitudes

Most Type A's are trying to prove something to themselves—and their world. What that is differs for each of us, though commonly Type A's are trying to prove they are not as useless and incompetent as they believe their parents or other significant people in their lives think they are. It doesn't really matter what the reason is—the outcome is the same.

Behind our attitudes are our beliefs—powerful beliefs about our self-worth, our calling, our dangers, and our fears of failure or success. The more we know about our deep-seated beliefs, the better we know ourselves.

Take time regularly to do a meaningful appraisal of your beliefs and attitudes. Ask, "What do I believe? What do I value? What do I want from life? What can I give? What can I change?" Write down a page of your thoughts in answer to each of these questions. Decide which are sensible and which are irrational, which are essential and which are non-essential.

Examine carefully your ethical and moral principles. Sure, you go to temple, church, or mass—but are you honest? Do you hurt others? Are you running away from your own evil? Is success all there is to your quest in life? If you were faced with a life-threatening crisis, would all you are currently striving for still seem important? Is there anything cluttering your everyday living that you would be better off without?

Of all the attitudes the Type-A person must challenge and change, the most important is the *attitude toward time*—particularly the sense of time urgency. This can lead to the "urgent" becoming a tyrannical master—with the Type-A person its slave.

About a year ago, a colleague and I were working very hard together on a project. It seemed very important to both of us that we get the job done. I remember telling him, "We need to get it done quickly!"

That evening I stood in the emergency room of our local hospital, confronted by my colleague's lifeless body. He had died that afternoon of a heart attack. Suddenly my "We need to get it done quickly" no longer had meaning. Death has a way of re-ordering priorities, and just seeing another person's life cut down before me forced me to take a serious look at my priorities.

Confronting death has a powerful way of changing our perspective. We move from a worm's-eye-view to a bird's-eye-view. But why do we wait until we catch a glimpse of the reality of eternity and our own human frailty before we respond with some sensible rearrangement of our attitude toward time?

Time-urgency is the essence of "hurry sickness." It is often irrational, compulsive, and eludes awareness. Only yesterday I needed a spare part for my car. I found myself saying, "I must stop what I am doing and go and get it *now*. I became tense, stressed, and bothered because something was waiting to be done, and I was so obsessed with doing it right away that I could not get my mind on other things. When I realized what I was doing, I reminded myself that the need really wasn't urgent at all, and talked myself out of a "hurry" episode.

Why are we so hurried and hassled? Why do we wish for thirty-six-hour days when we've only been given twenty-four? Why does the fierceness of our own hostility destroy us when it was designed to protect us? Why must we always prove to ourselves or others that we are perfect? There is only one answer to each of these questions, and it is for you to discover it for yourself!

Step 4: Change Your Behavior

When you have admitted your hurried tendencies and worked at changing your attitudes toward yourself and the world, then you are ready to change your behavior. Here are some guidelines:

- *Improve your time management.* Much hurry is caused by bad planning. For example, a few years ago I found I was always tense when I got to work. I had developed the habit of getting up rather late in the morning and not leaving enough time to complete my preparations before leaving for work. I would have to rush to the office in order to get there on time, and being "just in time" raised my stress level.

Rushing never allows you to eat a leisurely breakfast, read the paper, take a stroll in the garden, or "check up on the birds" before leaving home. Nor can you enjoy the slow lane on the freeway. You are forced to fight time when you don't allow enough of it for the essentials of life. Since discovering what a slave I had become to time, I have changed my behavior pattern. Now I get up a half-hour to forty-five minutes earlier than before. I take a leisurely bath instead of a hurried shower. I have time to read the newspaper and eat breakfast without feeling like I'm about to choke. I arrive at work calm and collected.

Try rising a little earlier than usual and see how much better you feel. If you need the extra sleep, add it to the front end—go to bed earlier.

Good time management means planning ahead. Don't be tyrannized by never having enough time to complete tasks and therefore always having to rush. Also, plan for time to be alone. Everyone needs time to collect the thoughts and restore balance to the values that really count.

Mothers can be especially stressed by all their responsibilities. Mothers who work outside the home tend to be even more stressed, especially when they don't receive much help from husbands.

If you are in this situation, it is especially important that you plan ahead. Make allowance for delays caused by others; start your chores well ahead of time. Use a work schedule if it will help you (perhaps it will impress your husband with how much you really do that he will begin to help). Show what must be done, and when. A little extra effort here will avoid those frantic, angry, nerve-destroying rushes that running out of time creates. You might also try *asking* for help; perhaps others in the family are not aware of how frantic you feel.

- *Slow down.* If you can plan ahead how you will use your time, you should be able to find time to slow down. But

even if you can't plan for it, slow down anyway. I don't recommend that you become lazy, and I certainly don't mean
you mustn't care about time. But it is a fact that most
people would be more efficient and effective if things were
done a little more slowly. This quick, impulsive way of
tackling tasks often means more mistakes, and tasks take
longer to accomplish.

One of my bad habits as a Type-A person is that I usually
believe I can carry everything that needs to be carried from
the car into the house *in one trip*. It's a challenge! Whether it
is the groceries from the supermarket, work projects from
my office, or tools after I have completed a repair, I always
believe I can save time by carrying everything in one trip. I
pile my arms high, hang bits over my shoulder, and thread
separate fingers through different objects—all to save time
by making just one trip.

I have never made it yet! I've tried dozens of times—without
success. I always drop something and it takes me much longer to
correct the situation than if I had simply decided to make two or
three trips. After all, its only about ten paces from where I park
my car to the front door!

Lately, I have deliberately tried to make two trips when I think
I can do it in one, or four trips if I think I should be able to carry
everything in two. I've chosen to do it this, simply for the self-
control it teaches. The result is that I feel less compulsive. I view
the extra walk as exercise and use it to unwind and enjoy the
garden.

In fact, I now try to take every opportunity I can to do incon-
sequential things the long way to retrain myself from always
being so hurried. And I am beginning to really *enjoy* slowing
down—although it was difficult at first! I choose the slow lane
on the freeway, the slow line in the supermarket, and the slow
movie on TV. Of course, I compensate for my usual hurrying by
going to the other extreme—and you may not need to go so far.
Perhaps by forcing myself to slow down drastically, I may achieve
enough balance so that in the future I don't have to think about
it so much.

I recommend you practice the following *new habits:*

- Speak more slowly and deliberately.
- Pause regularly between phrases.
- Learn to be a better listener.
- Walk more slowly.
- Don't do more than one thing at a time.
- Eat more slowly and savor your food.
- Drive more slowly.
- Do nothing for thirty minutes *every day.*

If we slow down our behaviors, we can slow down our metabolism and reduce our need for adrenaline.

- *Plan for fewer interruptions.* There are so many things that have the potential to interrupt us and keep us from developing a peaceful spirit: the telephone, kids, neighbors, dogs, salesmen—and even the postman. Not all these interruptions are necessary, and most put us on edge and irritate us. The resulting anger can often aggravate our "hurry sickness" and send us into an "emergency" mode of existence.

When I first began my practice as a clinical psychologist, clients had access to my home telephone number for emergencies. It was in the days before answering services or telephone answering machines came into being. It didn't take me long to become conditioned to the ring of the telephone so that I would jump whenever it rang. I started to hate the telephone; I would have nightmares about ringing telephones. The clanging of any bell that sounded like a telephone sent me into a cold sweat. Talk about conditioned responses! I felt like one of Pavlov's famous dogs. (Sorry, that's an inside joke among psychologists!)

The intrusion became intolerable, especially since most of the calls weren't emergencies at all.

I resolved the problem by eventually using an answering service when one opened up and having all calls screened. Most homes, I believe, would become more peaceful if they at least used an answering machine—or simply unplugged the phone during meal times. (I sometimes find myself wishing Alexander Graham Bell had not invented the telephone; it has become such an intrusively destructive instrument in the hands of those who do not have the courage to control it.)

Deal with other interruptions similarly. If you want time to yourself in the bedroom, hang out a sign saying "Do Not Disturb." If you want peace and quiet from noisy teenagers, take a walk in the park—and don't tell anyone *which* park!

Control your interruptions; *don't let them control you.* Refuse to answer the doorbell if you're busy (it's probably only a salesman). Let the telephone ring; you don't have to answer it every time. And be very clear in telling your family, coworkers, employees, or the gardener that you don't want to be interrupted. If you can do this, you can train your mind, body, and soul to become more peaceful.

- *Learn to laugh!* Type-A people hang onto the world as if their very life depended on it. They tend to take life too seriously, to believe they are indispensable and the world cannot function without them. They have trouble laughing at themselves. Some Type B's are not exactly the life of the party either, so we should all learn to lighten up!

Now, I am not advocating a denial of reality—far from it. There are certainly times when life's crises must be taken seriously, when there isn't time to laugh, or when it is time to cry. But how often is life really that serious? So your tire is flat—laugh! Then take out the jack and fix it. So the milk has boiled over—laugh! Then get the mop. So the dog has chewed up your favorite slippers—laugh! You needed a new pair anyway.

Try reacting to irritations by learning to see the humor in them. The power of humor to keep adrenaline low is quite remarkable. It is very hard to live in an "emergency mode" while you are seeing the funny side of things.

My two-year-old grandson, Vincent, reminded me of that one day. I was teaching him how to play with a toy I had bought him. It was an airplane that "flew" at the end of a thin cable, operated by a battery-driven motor held in the hand. We got it to work a few times, and he was thrilled. It flew round and round above his head as he dizzily turned with the cable.

Then it crashed. I mean, it really crashed! I thought the world was going to end. I was disappointed beyond words. We stood there, Vincent and I, looking at the several pieces of a once-magnificent flying machine, now scattered over the lawn. My brow was furrowed; my face was sad. He looked at the pieces, then at me, then back at the pieces—and started to laugh uproariously. My reaction to the "catastrophe" was apparently the funniest thing he had ever seen. He got pleasure out of the crash, as well as my reaction to it. All I got out of it was pain.

Then I started to laugh too, picked up the pieces, repaired the airplane, and we were once again in the flying business. Vincent's child-perspective helped me to see the catastrophe in a different light.

Laughter heals many things. It heals anger. Laughter creates love. Laughter restores perspective on life. Laughter creates cheerfulness in others. And the scientific validity of Proverbs 17:22 has long since been proven: "A cheerful heart does good like medicine, but a broken spirit makes one sick." There is now abundant evidence that two of the greatest stimulants to our immune system are humor and happiness. They are also good for high cholesterol, ulcers, and headaches.

So laugh. Out loud. Often. It's good for you, and it's *legal!* Norman Cousins said laughter is *inner iodine.* If that's true—and it is—we could all benefit from a few dozen doses of laughter each day.

Creativity and Stress

*What makes some people more creative than others? Why are
some able to be imaginative, innovative, trailblazers while the
rest struggle along in the same old ruts? Are creative people
born that way, or do they learn to be creative? Does it take a lot
of intelligence or hard work, or is it just luck or good fortune?*

For a long time I've been curious about the whole process of
what leads to or generates creative thought. I've watched a
friend produce whole stanzas of poetry while I struggle to find
a word to rhyme with "success." I've observed others jot down
the outline for a brilliant speech on the back of a napkin while
I soak up spilled coffee with mine. Am I envious? You can stake
your life on it!

"What have they got that I haven't got?" I've often wondered.
"Is it a special gift just given to them, or can anyone learn to be
more creative?" Not that I want to be a Mozart or an Einstein. I'm
not shooting for the stars. I just want creative thoughts to come a
little more easily so I can do the best that I can.

Because of this ongoing fascination with the creative mind and
how to nurse and nourish it, I have over many years carried out
an informal bit of research on myself. And in the process, I have
learned some interesting things about creativity and how I can
enhance it to my advantage. What I will share in this chapter,
therefore, has been proven through personal experience.

The most valuable thing I have learned in my personal exploration of creativity is that anybody—myself included—can learn to be more creative than they have been hitherto. Notice that I am choosing my words carefully. There is a limit to how much original creativity we can conjure up.

Intelligence and early training set up these limits. But be assured, all of us are a long way from these limits. We all function way below our true potential. This is not just a cliché, but a widely acknowledged fact. I have observed that under some conditions—for example in the dozy early hours of the morning—my mind is clearer, more crisp and innovative. Ideas come easily and I am able to organize them into coherent wholes more readily. Also, I have learned that there is a direct relationship between creativity and the level of my adrenaline arousal, which is why I am discussing this topic. Simply put, when I am most stressed I am least creative. High adrenaline dampens my creative juices as it prepares me for the more physical demands of the "fight or flight" response. A moment of personal reflection will probably confirm this in yourself as well.

This chapter is, therefore, devoted to an examination of how each of us can become more creative by learning new ways of thinking and by managing our stress to provide the optimal mental conditions for creative thought.

YOU CAN BE CREATIVE

As a psychologist, I have studied many aspects of human behavior. While much is known about how we think, there is still a lot of mystery surrounding the secrets of how some can turn on and sustain creative inspiration while others cannot. We know enough, however, to say to the many who have almost given up that a degree of creativity is something we can all experience—with a bit of practice.

This is not to say that anyone can be a genius if he or she so chooses. There are certain realms of invention that do seem to be reserved for just a few. But all of us can learn to open the creative doors a little wider and come up with new ideas or ways of doing things. We can do this in part by getting rid of negative and restrictive thinking habits that hinder the flow of creativity. But more importantly, we can become more spontaneous, inventive, and imaginative simply by learning to use the correct part of our brain—the so-called "right" side of the brain that has become identified with creativity.

Who needs to be more creative? I think we all do—some perhaps more than others. Ministers who must prepare interesting sermons, teachers who must instruct while maintaining interest and discipline, students who must complete projects or write papers and essays, homemakers who must make meager budgets stretch to create warm and inviting home conditions, engineers who must devise newer and more efficient ways to design bridges and dams, mechanics confronted with complex new technology—all these individuals could benefit from being more creative.

Beyond the work environment, creativity makes life more interesting and fulfilling. I believe it also places us in a more receptive frame of mind when relating to our spouses or family members, budgeting our resources, disciplining our children, or taking a vacation. Oh, yes! Let's not forget that it also makes us more interesting to be around. The most enjoyable people I know are also the most naturally creative.

WHAT IS CREATIVITY?

Simply put, creativity is the ability to do something differently or to bring something new into being. Creative thinking is a *special* form of thinking. We are all capable of it within certain limits, although it is to be expected that some will be a little more creative than others.

Creativity is a normal human capacity and everyone possesses the potential for more of it. From personal experience, I know that it can be cultivated and encouraged in all of us. The best analogy I can think of to illustrate the process is that of a garden. The mind is the garden that must be tilled, prepared, and cultivated before one can reap the benefit of one's labors. Creative thinking is a *reaping* of what one has *sown*. There can be no creative reaping if there has been no preparation of the mind's soil.

As we shall see, creativity is the outflow of good preparation and of being in the right frame of mind.

What is so special about creative thought?

- *It is novel.* It is a thought or thoughts that you haven't harvested before. It gives pleasure to yourself and others because it is a new way of thinking about or seeing something.

- *It is useful.* There is always some value in creativity. It helps us learn or solve problems—even personal problems—more efficiently. Or it can make us more sensitive to the beauty of the world around us.

- *It is synthetic.* It helps us combine separate ideas into meaningful "wholes." We gain greater perspective on life when we can see the larger picture.

- *It is solution-oriented.* When we think creatively, we come to a point of closure; we achieve resolution; we see the answers to complex questions more clearly.

- *It is beautiful.* It thrills and satisfies and gives life a rosy edge.

BLOCKS TO CREATIVITY

There are many "blocks" that can get in the way of the development and use of our creative abilities. By understanding and working to remove these blocks, we can enhance our creative functioning. Here are some of the common blocks to creative thinking:

- *Fear of making mistakes.* This inhibits new learning by reducing risk-taking. Creative people realize mistakes are inevitable, so they don't avoid taking action because they fear making them. They also know how to benefit from these mistakes.

- *Self-doubt.* This creates a negative mindset that prevents spontaneous and innovative actions. Creative people must have a fundamental belief in themselves, a belief that they are effective in what they do.

- *Fear of the unknown.* Most non-creative people do not want to leave the safety of their established ruts and non-effective ways of doing things. They prefer the shelter and safety of the known to the challenge of the unknown. Creative people, on the other hand, must be willing to engage the uncertain—at least, in certain areas of their lives. Unnecessary or stupid risk-taking is not what creative thinking is about.

- *Taking things too seriously.* Over-seriousness usually goes hand in hand with perfectionism. Together, these two attitudes tend to block creativity by emphasizing the preposterous need to be perfect and exaggerating the fear of failing. Creative people have "the courage to be imperfect" and enough of a humorous streak to laugh at themselves when they do fail.

Removing some of these blocks can help to enhance creativity, but this is not the whole story. Creativity is also a state of mind—a special way of thinking. And many of us have actually had this way of thinking almost "trained out of us" by our culture. There is much in our environment that discourages us from being creative!

A SPLIT BRAIN

As you may know, the brain is made up of two distinctive halves or hemispheres that are linked by a complex cable of nerves. Some researchers have tried to explain creative thinking by seeing it as a function of the "right" hemisphere of the brain rather than the "left." They point out that the brain is actually made up of two identical halves—identical up to a point, but with different realms under each hemisphere's control. For instance, the left half controls speech, language, logic, and reasoning. It is the "rational" half of the mind and it is the part that is most reinforced in our culture. We value the rational above the emotional or intuitive, so we constantly reinforce it by making it the trait that gets the best grades or earns the most money.

The right half of the brain, on the other hand, controls intuitive thinking. It helps us to value beauty, art, music, and wonderful sunsets. It is in the right hemisphere that creative thought arises. Actually, we always need both hemispheres and cannot do without either, but an over-controlled right side of the brain tends to suppress creativity. And we are not trained in the Western world on how to use this side of our brains. In fact, our educational system very much works against it!

For most of the time, our whole brain functions at its maximum capacity with both sides in full swing. But, according to the researchers, one or the other hemisphere may tend to dominate at a given time or in a given individual. (Each of the two halves is capable of functioning more or less on its own.) Now, the bad news is that our Western civilization has traditionally tended to value logic and rationality over intuitive thinking, and these are "left-brain" functions. Unfortunately, too much emphasis on left-brain activities can suppress or discourage the right brain, with its capacity for fantasy and innovative ways of looking at things, leaving us relatively non-creative and unimaginative. The good news is that even if you have spent your whole life training yourself in left-brain function, you can learn to open up your right side and discover intuitive, imaginative thoughts you never knew existed. I know. I've done it myself. I've gone from being a predominately left-brain, super-logical, rational person (my first career was as an engineer) to being more right-brain oriented. So it can be done!

How can we free up the more creative right side of the brain? The ideas suggested by educational researchers are very similar to the techniques I will describe in this chapter to help free the creativity locked within us, although to my knowledge no one has yet endeavored to show the connection I will try to make between low-levels of adrenaline arousal and creative thinking. Researchers talk of "creative inspiration" occurring during periods of being "unfocused" and in a state of "no demand." I think there is much truth to this. Whether or not this state is caused by right-brain dominance cannot be absolutely corroborated, but this is of little consequence to my recommendations for enhancing creativity. All we really need to know at this point is that good stress management is not only good for your health, but it also enhances creative thinking. We can leave the researchers to fight it out as to what actually goes on in the brain!

STRESS AND CREATIVE THINKING

What does creativity, or the lack of it, have to do with stress and adrenaline arousal? A lot—but not in the way we usually think.

Many of us hold to an erroneous belief that we are most creative at high levels of adrenaline arousal. We think that when we are feeling the best (which is usually when we are pumping enough adrenaline to light up New York), we are also at our most creative. But this is not so! In fact, a state of high arousal will almost certainly suppress creativity.

The connection between high stress and low creativity is well illustrated in one group of my patients. In my psychotherapy practice I see many clergy. I have a particular interest in how the role of the minister, priest, or rabbi creates a high state of stress that is counter-productive to creativity. In their preaching and teaching roles, clergy are called upon to be creative at all times. They must devise interesting sermon outlines, invent (or creatively "adapt") captivating illustrations, and all the time be true to what they preach. They must hold attention, yet communicate truth—and all within a twenty- or thirty-minute sermon which is all the average person in the pew will be able to absorb with their limited attention spans. It is quite a challenging task! I've tried it, so I know.

Most clergy find sermon preparation to be difficult, tedious work, although they do enjoy the preaching. Invariably when I ask when and how they set about their preparation, I discover it is usually during periods of high adrenaline arousal. They often "psych" themselves up and ingest large amounts of coffee before they can get going and feel creative.

Is this helpful in fostering creativity? Not at all. They actually make it harder on themselves, because creative thought occurs best at low, not high, levels of arousal! So don't confuse the exciting, energizing feelings of high adrenaline with being most creative.

General adrenaline arousal can be seen as falling into three levels:

- *Low arousal.* In this state, the mind is awake but not "in gear;" it is idling like a well-tuned engine without consuming vast quantities of fuel. The mind is relatively "unfocused" in a way that opens up all of its memory and resources; it can digest thoughts and engage freely in uninhibited, free-flowing thought. Low arousal is also a state of reverie and daydreaming; it is while we are in this state that memory recall and intuitive thinking are enhanced. This is the state in which we achieve maximum creativity, as many writers will attest.

- *Medium arousal.* In a medium level of arousal, the mind is wide awake and active. The body is adequately aroused and prepared for moderate action.

In this state one can concentrate and not be distracted, but there is no anxiety; planning is efficient during such a stage. A good example of such a stage is what you may experience when working on your income taxes. There is an alertness which comes from the threat of making mistakes, and an efficiency that calculating and reasoning demands. But your creative abilities are somewhat reduced. You are concentrating only on the task before you, so you don't have any free-floating thought activity. Medium arousal, then, is the stage of maximum receptivity to information and ideas, but not to the generation of artistic or fertile creative thought.

- *High arousal.* At this stage, the mind is in high gear; it is highly alert and reactive. Adrenaline flows more strongly than in the medium stage and there is a physical and mental restlessness prompting one to action. You can see it in people's behavior. They pace up and down, back and forth. They tap their foot and even become easily irritated, because they are in a state of readiness to attack or defend themselves.

At high arousal, decisions are made more rapidly and action responses are almost purely reflexive. The mind is highly focused on the immediate task, and cuts out all extraneous stimuli, even to the extent of obliviousness to sounds and movement. The brain's total attention is focused on the problem or demand immediately at hand. Memory recall is slow and difficult because the urgent task demands attention.

This stage of arousal borders on and may even include the "fight or flight" response. There is only one level of arousal above this stage—namely panic, especially panic anxiety attack. This level is beyond the scope of my discussion here, but it is a state in which all memory is blocked, name recall is difficult, and basic survival is the only function of the brain.

High arousal is the stage of efficient *action* but of inefficient creativity, for the obvious reason that the brain is focused on engagement, not disengagement.

So, as we move along this continuum from low arousal through medium to high arousal, we see that the mind and body move from a state of unfocused disengagement with maximum recall, to one which is highly focused on action but not on recall. It goes from creative preparedness to "fight or flight" and ultimately panic. At low arousal, adrenaline discharge is minimal. At high arousal, it is maximal.

There is also a change in the brain's electrical activity as we move from low to high arousal. At low arousal, brain waves are slow, bordering on drowsiness. The patterns they produce are called "theta" waves. At medium arousal, brain waves are typical of wakefulness and are called "alpha" waves. At high arousal, brain waves become faster and attention is highly focused. High-arousal brain waves are called "beta" waves.

The less aroused one is, the greater the number of theta waves produced. The more aroused one becomes, the greater the alpha, then beta waves and the fewer theta waves produced by the brain. This understanding of how the electrical activity of the brain fluctuates with the level of adrenaline arousal has led to the development of biofeedback techniques used for training people to produce theta or even alpha waves, which are considered to be basic for creative thinking.

We can all learn to lower our level of arousal to utilize the state of increased creativity without resorting to the use of expensive biofeedback equipment. How can we do this? I will devote the remainder of this chapter to addressing this question.

USING LOW AROUSAL TO ENHANCE CREATIVITY

There is now abundant evidence that our most inventive and creative state of mind is at low levels of adrenaline arousal. Contrary to what many people believe, it is when we are minimally aroused by adrenaline that we do our most innovative and imaginative thinking.

In psychology, there is a principle known as the "Yerkes-Dodson Law" (named after those who first formulated it), which states that there is an "inverted-U" relationship between arousal of the mind and body and the efficiency with which we can perform certain tasks. This law essentially states:

1. At low arousal, we are not very effective in action tasks but very good at thinking creatively.

2. As arousal increases (medium arousal), we become more effective in action but less effective in creative thinking.

3. As arousal becomes very high, our efficiency in both action and thinking drops off again. This is probably the stage of "panic" when all systems shut down.

The Yerkes-Dodson Law, then, is highly consistent with the model I have just presented, concerning how adrenaline levels influence creativity. High arousal forces people to move away from creative and innovative thought because in the emergency facing them they are forced back to old, familiar ways of doing things. They tend to panic and act on old reflexes instead of forge ahead with new thinking.

Of course, once we have done our creative work and our ideas have been formulated at low levels of arousal, we must be able to move to a higher level of arousal in order to put our thoughts into action. In a sense, therefore, we need both low and medium levels of arousal for effective living. Seldom do we need a very high level of arousal in modern-day living. It should be reserved for genuine emergencies and kept to a minimum. Living constantly at a high level of arousal, which is common for Type-A people, is clearly damaging because of the stress disease it fosters.

Let me illustrate how creative thinking at low levels of arousal occurs in everyday life and experience, so you can recognize it when it is happening and understand how it works.

Have you ever struggled to recall a name? These days, I seem to be having more and more trouble with name recall! Perhaps during a conversation with a friend you reminisced about old times and mentioned "old so-and-so," then couldn't recall his or her name. Or when cleaning out a cupboard, you placed a golf club or gadget in some special place and later couldn't remember where you put it. You struggled hard, trying to force your gray cells to do their best and restore the memory of the name or place . . . but to no avail. Memory eluded you. And the harder you struggled to remember, the more elusive the thing you were trying to recall became.

Finally, you just gave up and forgot about it. You went to bed. As drowsiness set in, the memory suddenly popped into your head. The name of your old friend or the place where you put that golf club was suddenly crisp and clear.

Or perhaps it was in the early hours of the next morning while you lay awake, trying to fall back into the delicious arms of slumber. In that unguarded, low-aroused moment, your memory came leaping back at you.

What happened? By becoming drowsy, you fell into a state of low arousal. You triggered some "theta" waves, and in this state, you unlocked the full power of your memory. You were able to access all of your mind, not just a limited part of it as happens when you become alerted. Your thoughts were relatively unfocused and in this state the channel to your brain cells opened and memory became fully functioning. In fact, inhibitory circuits in the brain helped shut out extraneous activity at higher arousal states, which is why your memory was less available—all very wonderfully designed, when you think about. No humanly designed computer could compare with our magnificent brains.

I have solved many problems—problems that have bugged me for hours during my waking state—just when I am about to fall asleep. My research work often requires that I write a computer program. As any programmer will tell you, there is always a lot of debugging to do. No program runs just as you want it to—not mine, at least. Many evenings are spent, struggling to get a program to "run" and trying to find the bug in it when it won't run. Usually, the more frustrated I become (adrenaline going up), the more the solution eludes me. I am well-equipped to kick the computer, but not to create a solution.

Finally, after I've resigned myself to not being able to solve the problem, I go to bed . . . to "sleep on it." Inevitably, I wake up early the next morning with the solution to the error staring me in the face.

As I slept and lowered my alertness, my mind opened up its creativity channels and presented me with the solution. No struggle. Just relaxing was enough to open up the full power of the mind.

Try this experiment tonight. As you lie down to sleep, prompt your mind to help you recall some early event in your life. Choose a period of your life you have long since forgotten. As you relax and prepare to go to sleep, try to recall something that happened at this stage of life so as to fix an anchor point. Remind yourself of some incident when you were five or six years old. Then wait. Just relax and don't try to force any memory. Soon your mind will present you with another memory, then another—events you haven't remembered for years will begin to come back to you.

It is remarkable what we can recall if we prompt our memory during a state of low adrenaline arousal. Often in my therapy with patients who have been abused in early childhood I use this "drowsy recall" technique to help them uncover and deal with unpleasant early experiences that have been "buried" for years. Such recall of early life events—whether they are traumatic or not—can be very therapeutic. Early life joys as well as hurts can come to light.

STEPS IN THE CREATIVE PROCESS

There are four steps that can be used to enhance your creative thinking, using a low state of adrenaline arousal. In explaining them, I will use the analogy of a garden because I think it beautifully and most accurately illustrates the process. The steps are these:

1. Prepare the soil of your mind by *tilling* it.

2. Implant ideas in your mind from which creative thoughts can emerge by *seeding* this tilled soil.

3. Allow the seeds of thought to develop and come to fruition by giving them time to *germinate.*

4. Finally, glean the benefits of creative seeding by reaping.

I can best illustrate this creative process by providing a brief explanation of how I have used these four simple steps to enhance my own creative ability. I know they work because I use them all the time and have taught them to people in many walks of life.

TILLING THE SOIL OF YOUR MIND

In any garden, the most important preparation is the removal of those contaminating influences that would inhibit the growth of new plants—weeds, rocks, insects, and so on. In the garden of the creative mind, the equivalent contaminants are such mental activities as faulty beliefs, inhibitory thought patterns, and pre-conditioned or biased ideas.

Some of us just think too negatively. We've been told—and we now believe without question—that we can't solve problems or think of new ideas. So we never try.

Children are not born thinking this way. They must learn it. They are taught by negative-thinking parents, who learned it from their parents. Children have an instinctive "pipeline to creativity" that can easily be shut off by cynical parents. By the same token, healthy thinking patterns can be encouraged.

I dabble a little in conjuring and sleight of hand. It makes for being a great grandfather, because I always have exciting ways to entertain my grandchildren! And I have always been fascinated by the magician who can fool anyone—including me—into believing he's worked a miracle, simply because his hand is faster than my eye. Years ago, I used to do my magic act for Sunday school parties and was able to use it very effectively in talks to children. What always puzzled me, however, was how easy it was to fool the adults but how quickly the younger members of my audience saw through my tricks. The younger the children, the more difficult they were to fool! Why are adults easier to fool? Because they are full of preconceived ideas that have been drummed into their minds. So they believe almost any of my misdirections. But young children don't have those preconceived notions, so they see things more creatively—including how to figure out "where the bunny went."

We *till* our minds and prepare them for creative thought by undoing some of the preconceived, negative thinking patterns of the past. We must deliberately open ourselves to new ideas and avoid making assumptions based on past experiences. When faced with a problem, we will be able to solve it more creatively if we say to ourselves, "I will open my mind to new ways of looking at this." Even when we've tried to solve a dilemma a dozen times before, we must continue to open our minds to new possibilities by saying, "I'm going to approach this problem with a fresh mind and perhaps see a solution this time."

Creative people, you see, don't let the past deter them from thinking new ideas or new ways of doing things. They don't give up if things seem impossible. They're always willing to try and try again. They see problems as challenges to new thinking, are open-minded, force themselves to see the world differently, keep an optimistic outlook at all times, and consequently are ready to receive creative inspiration.

While naturally creative people do this unconsciously, all of us can learn to be this way by consciously and repetitively reminding ourselves of the value of these attributes. This is how we till the mind to make it receptive to new ideas. Doing it frequently softens our rigidity, creates an explorer's mindset, and removes the old, inhibiting, negative thought patterns.

Seeding Your Mind

Creative thinking never occurs in a vacuum. Gardens grow beautiful foliage and flowers because someone planted and tended the seed that was sown.

One reason so many never feel creative is that they do not plant enough *seed* in their minds. Creative people are that way because they have taken the time to study, read, and expose their minds to a broad base of input information. Then they merely reap what they have sown.

The creative public speaker, for instance, is brilliant not because she was born with an encyclopedia of ideas in her head; she has spent time cultivating her mind by reading widely the topics she knows people want to hear about. Then she simply reaps what she has sown.

The creative musician has spent thousands of hours practicing; the creative writer has written a phrase a dozen times so as to perfect it; the creative teacher has also done her homework. These creative individuals merely reap what they have sown.

Seeding the mind can take many forms. If I am preparing to write a paper for presentation at a conference, for days or even weeks ahead of time I seed my mind by reading as much as I can about the topic. I talk to others about it, bouncing ideas off them in order to clarify my own thinking. Seeding can also take the form of thinking or reasoning with myself about an issue. While there is a limit to how much sense I can make out of a conversation with myself, it can be very helpful to mentally go over all the different points of view I can think of.

Seeding of the mind can best take place during medium levels of arousal. You need to be alert, attentive, somewhat focused, and in a learning mode. Remember, you are taking in, not putting out.

The essential point about creativity is that you can only get out what you put in. This is not to say that what you produce won't be your own—or won't be creative. It will. But it may come out in some new form, or may be a creative extension into some new way of seeing an old idea. Perhaps you may discover an insight that is totally new and creative.

Let me illustrate how the seeding of your mind works. Suppose you have to prepare a speech or sermon. You have chosen a topic but you're not sure how to present your ideas in an intriguing way. So you begin seeding your mind; you read all the background material you can get your hands on early in the week. You memorize the portion of Scripture you will preach on. In other words, you steep yourself in every available resource you have at hand until your mind is bathed in your topic. Now you are ready to let your ideas *germinate,* which is the third step in the creative process.

ALLOWING YOUR THOUGHTS TO GERMINATE

After you have reviewed, read, or listened to as much as you can about the issue at hand, you will need to leave it alone for awhile so that it can *germinate*. Without being aware of it, your mind will continue to digest, order, play with, examine, and ruminate on your seeded ideas. You may sometimes catch yourself thinking about the subject, but a lot of the germination goes on without your being consciously aware of it. This period is extremely important, and the most neglected, in the creative process. It is equivalent to allowing bread to rise before baking or fruit to ripen before you eat it!

Most of us need at least one or two days for our "thought seeds" to germinate before we can expect any creative thought. And different people find different activities conducive to the germination process. I prefer to sleep on my seeds. During the night my mind works without my knowing it, digesting the material, enlarging my brain's involvement. Others like to go for a walk, paint a house, or jog. Winston Churchill used to lay bricks; Ernest Hemingway went for early morning strolls before he sat down to write; and Carl Jung, the famous psychologist, took afternoon naps as a precursor to his creative time. Any form of distraction can facilitate this unconscious digestion of ideas that will lead to the next step in the creative process.

The germination of ideas is best accomplished during low levels of adrenaline arousal. This is why so many anecdotes about the creativity of some genius or other often include references about that person's sleeping or napping habits. Without always understanding what they were doing, these great minds developed a habit of establishing a state of low arousal during which the germination of their ideas took place.

REAPING YOUR CREATIVE THOUGHTS

Reaping can only occur after properly tilling the mind, seeding it with background material, and allowing it all to germinate. Reaping is best carried out during a low to medium state of arousal. I prefer it to be as low as possible!

It is here that most people make their greatest mistakes, then wonder why they never feel creative. You can never reap what you haven't sown, and you cannot reap when you are highly aroused. Once your system has become adrenally excited, creative reaping becomes almost impossible. You are in "fight or flight" mode, not reflective or creative mode.

I prefer my reaping to take place in the first hours of the day. This is when I do my best writing or creative brainstorming. I get up early and before I bathe or even eat, I sit down with pen and paper and begin to write down my ideas. I avoid coffee or other stimulants because I know they will elevate my adrenaline and cut back the little creativity I have. Perhaps very creative Type-B people don't have to manage themselves like this, but I do. And, I suspect, so do many of my readers.

I do my creative work before my other work—whether it be teaching, seeing patients, or administration—because once I get to my office and start my daily routine, my adrenaline starts to flow quite strongly and I become more alert and energized. This is helpful for action-oriented activities. I become very efficient. But my real creative ability declines. I am too "wired" and restless to be contemplative. The demands and pressures of the day kill the little bit of novel thought I might otherwise possess.

WHEN CREATIVITY IS BLOCKED

Everyone at one time or another has experienced "writer's block"—that dreaded and mysterious shutting off of creative ideas. For the school teacher, it may be a lack of incentive to teach; for the musician, it could be a loss of memory for where the fingers must go at what time. The writer knows it well—he becomes frozen to the chair or paces the floor like a caged tiger trying to get enough fresh ideas to write. Try as he may, nothing—I mean nothing—comes to mind. The pen (or these days, the computer) lies idle, the paper starts to yellow, and the coffee flows by the gallon. Hour after hour, the mind seems barren.

There are many reasons why writers get these blocks. They are the same reasons why anyone who must be creative occasionally becomes blocked. Here are a few of them:

- Sometimes the problem is simply fatigue. We need to put down pen, chalk, or violin and get some sound and solid rest.

- Sometimes the block is caused by over-practice. Sportsmen and women know this well. Too much training can stifle creativity.

- Sometimes the level of adrenaline arousal is too high and we need to back off and lower our arousal again. Stress, especially, can cause us to stay at high arousal.

Whatever the reason, the solution is to go back to the beginning of the creative process and start the "tilling," "seeding," and "germinating" sequence over again. Or, to change the metaphor, if we have run out of creative thought, it could be that the "barrel" of our mind has simply run dry and needs refilling.

Also, if we wait too long between germinating a set of ideas and reaping them, we can lose what we have sown through the process of forgetting. The ideas are lost before we can reap. For instance, three months before Christmas I was asked to write an article for a magazine on the topic of why people become depressed during the holiday season. I did my research and read a few other articles to "seed" my mind. Then I waited to allow some germination but didn't get back to the project until two weeks later. When I sat down and tried to write the article, nothing—and I mean *nothing*—came out! I started, tore up the sheet, and started again. It was hopeless. I had waited too long between sowing and reaping, and as in the parable of the sower, the birds of time had snatched my seeds of thought away.

How did I overcome this block? I went back to the beginning and reread the background material for the topic—reseeding my mind. Two days later, the writing was a breeze and I finished it in less than an hour. I had sown, germinated, and reaped in timely fashion and took great pleasure in producing my own creation.

So can you—if you understand the relationship between creativity and adrenaline arousal.

Spiritual Antidotes for Stress

To this point, I have refrained from making too many comments about how our spiritual life affects the stress we experience. I am aware that many readers may not have any interest in such a topic.

If this is so, then I trust that what you have read thus far has sufficiently helped you to become a more peaceful, less stressed person. However, I would invite you to read this closing chapter, if only to get a sense of where I am coming from. Even though your religious beliefs may differ from mine, you should still find what I have to say beneficial.

For the many of my readers who do have an interest in spiritual matters, however, I would like to end this book with a discussion of how the spiritual side of our being interacts with the physical and psychological to produce, or relieve, stress. I happen to believe that we have many spiritual resources that can help us here. For some, regrettably, *religion is more of a stress producer than reliever.* It places demands or restrictions on them that might be more frustrating than beneficial, more burdensome than extricating, more oppressive than liberating. If this is true for you, I hope that what I have to say will help you to reorient your spiritual life so that it can become a healthier, more significant part of your existence.

My experience as a Christian believer has never been anything but positive and wholesome. I have, however, both through my professional work as a clinical psychologist as well as through personal acquaintance, come across many whose religious experiences have been less than health producing for them. Their beliefs were all form with no substance or life! They were more preoccupied with keeping the rules of their faith than with living a life of wholeness.

Not all religions—or denominations of the Christian faith, for that matter—are wholesome or helpful when it comes to protecting us from stress disease. Some forms of religion oppress women. Others foster racism or exclusivism, a form of religious apartheid based upon beliefs of superiority. Some demand uncritical allegiance, often to the whims of a maniacal tyrant. There are many second-league Jim Joneses or David Koreshes out there working their destruction on unsuspecting followers. Others, less dramatic in their style, preach and impose unreasonable standards on ordinary people, standards that guarantee a perpetual feeling of inadequacy in their followers of maintaining their allegiance. The abusive inculcation of neurotic guilt in unsuspecting devotees has to be the greatest source of emotional abuse and stress perpetrated in the name of religion that I know of. While I cannot address myself to all these concerns, I do want to point the way to a healthier spirituality by highlighting several important principles that should characterize it. I will discuss these principles primarily with regard to the *Christian faith* because I am not experienced in dealing with the psychological problems generated by other faiths. A complete treatment of how many forms of religion can be destructive, interesting as it might be, could be the topic of a book all to itself.

FAITH AND STRESS

In the final analysis, good stress management is as much a matter of spirituality as it is of self-discipline and mastery over our bodies. Religious faith plays a major role in how we create and respond to stress because it influences our values and priorities. Our life as faithing persons can protect us from much distress, or it can be the cause of high stress. The message of a healthy faith is tailored to *suit the needs of our whole being,* whereas the import of an unhealthy faith is destructive. When we entrust ourselves to a wholesome faith, we find shelter and safety from our troubled worlds.

How can we discover and develop a faith that is healthy and fosters protection from stress and distress? Let me begin by reviewing the life of Jesus to see what it can tell us about the *spiritual antidotes for stress.* Thereafter, I will expand on some important principles that are essential to creating a composed life for yourself.

JESUS—THE MODEL OF A STRESS-FREE LIFE

Even a cursory reading of the Gospels will show that the life of Jesus was a model of calmness and composure—the very opposite of what most of us experience in our hassled and hurried existences. Look at Him asleep at the back of a ship, as described in Mark 4:38. A great storm comes up, with waves beating into the ship so that it is swamped with water. Jesus goes on sleeping! Was He oblivious to the storm? I doubt it. Was He inconsiderate of the peril that faced them all? Absolutely not. When the disciples woke Him and asked, "Master, carest thou not that we perish?," He not only calmed the sea but asked them, "Why are ye so fearful? How is it that ye have no faith?" (v. 40). This challenge suggests that our lack of faith must be behind most, if not all, our fears.

What sort of life did Jesus model for us? First, I would say that His life was a model of *unhurriedness.* One could argue that unhurriedness was characteristic of Jewish life in New Testament times, but I think there is more to it than this. A life of perfect faith— faith that understands that God is in control even when nature is turbulent—cannot be anything but a life of peace.

The life of Jesus was also a model of *balanced priorities.* We see this in the story of Mary and Martha, sisters who had received Jesus into their home (Luke 10:38–42). Martha, who was probably the older, was so caught up with the importance of their visitor that she went into quite a dither about getting things just right. "Where's the wine? Who knocked the jug over? Do you have to make extra work for me? What should I cook for dinner? I just know that the butcher has sent me bad meat again! Whatever will *He* think if I don't make everything just perfect? I'm sure He thinks I'm a rotten housekeeper! If only they'd have given me more notice of His coming to visit. . . ."

And so on. It's really not that much different today, is it?

Finally, after she could take no more, Martha accused Jesus of not caring about how hard she was working and how He was allowing Mary, her layabout and irresponsible sister, to just sit at His feet and soak up all His teaching.

"Tell her to help me," she blurts out. "We won't eat until midnight if we don't get a move on. Shake her to her senses and get her to lend a helping hand!"

I'm embellishing a little, of course, but this was the gist of her attack on Jesus and her sister.

Listen to the patient and perspective-restoring reply of Jesus: "Martha, Martha, thou art careful and troubled about many things: but one thing is needful: and Mary hath chosen that good part which shall not be taken away from her."

We're not told how Martha took these words of admonishment. Perhaps she threw down her dish cloth and stormed out of the house in anger. Perhaps she did the passive anger thing, went silent, hid in a corner, and pouted the rest of the day. Who knows! But I like to think she did the mature thing and calmly put down the pot she was holding, took off her apron, pulled up a pillow, and sat down right there next to Mary at the feet of Jesus. Perhaps they didn't even bother to eat that day; perhaps they gave the food prepared for Jesus to the poor. After all, food cannot be all that important when you have an opportunity to sit before the Messiah and hear the words of God being spoken!

Keeping the *Jesus model* of unhurriedness and balanced priorities in mind, I would like to suggest a little exercise that you could do once every month, or every several months, to help you become aware of the priorities that are driving your life. Take pen and paper and imagine that you are Mary or Martha sitting at the feet of Jesus. Imagine that He asks you to write down on your list everything you are trying to accomplish at this time in your life. Then go on to list your disappointments, your uncompleted projects and unrealized dreams. Ask yourself whether any of these are *really that important*. If they are not, cross them off your list—and forget about them!

Then prioritize your goals for the next month or two. Ask yourself, "What would Jesus want me to do first? What would He want me to forget? Who would He like me to forgive?"

The object of the exercise is to increase your awareness of what needs to be done and to establish clearer, more balanced goals for your life. More importantly, it is to help you be clearer about *what really matters*. So, put down your pots and pans and sit at the feet of Jesus for awhile and do some deep heart searching about your priorities.

Now, let me turn your attention to two spiritual principles that I believe can provide an effective antidote for stress. There are others also, but space limitation forces me to confine my remarks to these two.

SPIRITUAL RESOURCES FOR COPING WITH PEOPLE

We saw in an earlier chapter that *people* are one of the primary causes of stress in most of our lives. But we also saw that we need people—or at any rate, we can't avoid them. So how can we deal more effectively with people, yet keep our stress under control?

I believe the Bible holds out two very important principles which, if followed, can minimize the stress of dealing with people:

1. The "Love Principle"

Is there any principle of Christian living more emphasized by Jesus, who said, "Your strong love for each other will prove to the world that you are my disciples" (John 19:95, LB).

The role of love in reducing stress can be quite remarkable, but many people are still unsure what it means to love. There are three common misconceptions about love that seem to get in the way of being a loving person:

Misconception Number 1: Love is only a feeling.

Because we are so preoccupied as a culture with romantic love, it is universally believed that love is a *feeling*. True, there is a "feeling" component that eventually comes, but it is a mistake to see love as only a feeling. Mature love is not just a feeling, but a *set of behaviors*. In the Bible, this fact is clearly pointed out in that well-known description of love found in 1 Corinthians, chapter 13. In it, love is depicted as behavior—how we treat one another. If I am patient, kind, never jealous nor envious, not proud, selfish, or rude—then I am loving another.

So where do love feelings come in? Love feelings are the *consequences*, not the origin, of loving acts. They are the reward for loving behavior. In other words, when I behave toward someone else in a loving way, I soon begin to feel love for that person. I have taught many married couples this principle, couples who allege that they no longer have love feelings for each other. I ask them to begin *behaving* toward each other in loving ways. Treat your partner with respect. Take flowers home. Open car doors—you know the sort of thing! It usually works like a miracle. In a matter of a week or two, love feelings come flooding back. Try the experiment for yourself!

Now there is one very important implication for this principle. It means that it is possible to love *before* you feel any good feelings about someone. If love is first behavior, then we don't have to wait until we *feel* love before we *begin* to love. On reflection, I am sure you will see the value of this. If we always had to feel love *before* we behaved in a loving way, others would have a long time to wait! Some would have to wait forever!

Misconception Number 2: Loving is the same as liking.

Our lives are full of people we dislike and don't enjoy. For many years, it bothered me because there were so many people I didn't like. I didn't hate them, I just didn't care to be around them that much. Some were neighbors, some were coworkers, some were just casual acquaintances. I felt guilty because it seemed to me that I ought to like everyone. Isn't that what God expects of us? Now I am wiser. I am so thankful that God doesn't tell us to like everyone—only to love them. And *liking* and *loving* are not one and the same thing.

It works this way: If I *like* you, chances are that I am already doing loving things for you. It's when I *don't* like you that I have a problem. Now, there is no natural loving instinct at work, prompting me to be patient, kind, or respectful. It is here that the commandment of Jesus to "love our enemies" (Matt. 5:44) makes sense. I can *love* my enemy who is, by definition, someone I don't *like* because love is a set of behaviors, not a feeling. Obviously, if someone is our "enemy," he or she is hardly someone we would like. But loving does not require us to like, only to behave in a loving way.

And here also, a miracle takes place. I have proven it to myself many times. If there is someone in my life that I dislike intensely, I set about behaving toward that person in a loving way. I begin by showing respect. I follow up with an occasional kind deed or compliment. Soon, a change begins to occur. My dislike begins to shift. I begin to enjoy the person I once avoided. Soon we are the greatest of friends. So we must stop letting our dislike of people get in the way of our loving them. We may even discover that others will begin to like us more if we change our behavior.

Misconception Number 3: Loving is the opposite of hating.

It is a very common belief that love and hate are opposites. We commonly believe that if we feel hate for someone, it means we couldn't possibly love them.

True? Not at all! Love and hate may feel different, but they *are not opposites*. *Love* and *fear* are opposites. When I am afraid of someone, love goes out the window. Love and indifference are opposites. To be indifferent to your children is a sure sign you don't love them. But love and hate are *two sides of the same coin*. They are two expressions of a very deep caring about another person.

In fact, intense hate is often a symptom of a deep love that has been thwarted or rejected. As the song goes: "You always hate the one you love." If you hate with a deep passion, chances are that your feeling comes from wanting to love that person more deeply, but not being allowed to.

True, there are hate feelings that have no basis in a thwarted love. Just as love and hate can be two sides of the same coin, hate can be linked with fear, resentment, or a deep feeling of injustice. Help for such hate may not be possible through the *love principle* by itself. Something has to happen *before* love can be invoked, and this will be the focus of the next principle I will discuss.

2. The "Forgiveness Principle"

Love and forgiveness are closely linked in Scripture. To love is always to forgive. *Not to forgive is not to love.* Very often, forgiveness has to precede the freedom to love.

The ability to forgive is, therefore, a very important stress reliever. Those who can't forgive and who harbor resentments are likely to be those who carry the greatest stress. When the mind perceives the need for revenge or defense, it keeps the alarm system at a high state of readiness—adrenaline flows abundantly!

Freedom from the destructive force of anger is only possible through two mechanisms: *revenge* or *forgiveness.* Since revenge is not always possible or desirable, forgiveness is the only way out of the prison of resentment.

I doubt if a deeply forgiving person ever suffers from severe stress disease. There is something about a forgiving spirit that restores the brain's tranquillity and lowers the "fight or flight" response. Of course, anger is not the only cause of stress damage, but it certainly is a significant one. So being able to forgive those who cause us hurt can keep us free from a lot of distress.

Because forgiveness is such an important spiritual antidote for stress, I would like to emphasize a few basic but important points about it. Again, my goal is to challenge those basic misconceptions that keep us doing the wrong things. Here are some important points to keep in mind in an effort to become a more forgiving person:

- Forgiveness *does not condone* the nasty behavior of those needing our forgiveness. It merely stops the cycle of attack and counter-attack, hurt and revenge.

- Forgiveness does not let the perpetrator of your hurt go free. *It leaves justice in God's hands.*

- Forgiveness *protects the forgiver* from the harm done to himself or herself by unresolved anger.

- Forgiveness is always for the *forgiver's benefit*, not just for the one needing the forgiveness.

- Forgiveness *does not need the other person to acknowledge* the harm he or she has done.

- Forgiving others is the other side of being forgiven by God. It is one of the *conditions of God's covenant* with us.
- Forgiveness is a *special gift God offers us* for healing our deep-seated resentments, whether or not the hurts we experience are deserved.

But forgiveness isn't always easy. Why, then, should we become generous forgivers? The following story may help you understand the importance of forgiveness as you struggle to find a pathway for yourself.

A patient once shared with me a long list of deep resentments. And, as you will see, she has had more than her fair share of life's hurts. Her birth parents abandoned her as a baby because they wanted "to be free." Her adoptive parents were cruel and abusive. An uncle raped her when she was nine. As an adolescent she developed a bad skin condition that turned friends away and made her feel like a misfit. Even though she is quite intelligent she has never felt able to accomplish a significant educational goal. Her first husband abandoned her for another woman. And the list goes on and on. In fact, the only positive aspect of this woman's life was a faint, but stubborn, hope in a God who just might care a little bit about her. At least, belief in God gave her someone to blame!

As you can imagine, this woman had a lot of deep-seated anger—anger at the world, at herself, and at the God she hoped was really there.

"What can I do?" she asked with tears of anguish streaming down her face.

"Let me help you discover the liberating power of forgiveness," I whispered, with a few tears of my own trickling down my cheeks.

"I think God has already prepared the way for your healing," I told her. "He must have known that sooner or later someone with just the messed-up and unfair sort of life you've experienced was going to come along, because he worked out all the details for you." I then went on to explain that secular psychology really has no solution for resolving the deep hurts and resentment caused when life has been so unreasonable and lopsided in dispensing unfair pain and suffering. There is no human resource to heal such hurt. It turns most people into bitter, alienated human beings. Only God has the answer to such unfairness; not psychology nor a hundred years of psychotherapy! I read her Matthew 5:38–48:

> "The law of Moses says, "If a man gouges out another's eye, he must pay with his own eye. If a tooth gets knocked out, knock out the tooth of the one who did it." But I say—don't resist violence! If you are slapped on one cheek, turn the other too. If you are ordered to court and your shirt is taken from you, give your coat too. If the military demand that you carry their gear for a mile, carry it two. Give to those who ask, and don't turn away from those who want to borrow. There is a saying, "Love your friends and hate your enemies." But I say: Love your enemies! Pray for those who persecute you! In that way you will be acting as true sons of your Father in heaven."

Many scoff at the idea of "turning the other cheek," but the principle of forgiveness set out here is profound in its effect on dissolving vindictiveness. Jesus reminds us here that under the old law, the rule of life was simple: If someone hurt you, you were entitled to hurt that person back. *An eye for an eye and a tooth for a tooth* was the law of survival and punishment. But He takes us beyond that old law, which never really worked anyway, because if someone took out your eye you would not be content with just taking one of his—you would want both.

Psychologically, revenge never satisfies unless it gives more than it receives. So Jesus says, "If someone hurts you on the right cheek, turn the left also." Why? Turn your cheek because it is the only way to break the cycle of wanting revenge for your hurt.

Oh, how we misunderstand Jesus and balk at His wisdom! Our lower nature wants revenge, not to be hurt more. Turning the other cheek seems like the act of a coward. "They'll just stomp all over me again," is what most of us cry back to Jesus. "They'll get away without being punished." Heaven forbid that anyone should get away with causing us hurt!

God knows that it is our natural tendency to seek revenge. He also knows that the chain of revenge never ends. If I take out your eye, then you will want to take out mine; I will then want your other eye, and you will retaliate with my remaining eye. The result: we will both be blind, and neither will be satisfied. The cycle of revenge never ends—it only causes wars, as trouble spots around the world can attest. This is why we need a better way—the *way of forgiveness.*

After telling us in Ephesians 4:26 that we can be angry but should not sin, Paul also goes on to tell us: "Stop being . . . angry. . . . Instead, be kind to each other, tenderhearted, forgiving one another" (Eph. 4:31–32, lb).

So why should I forgive those who have unjustifiably hurt me? I forgive them because I need to protect myself from my own revenge. I forgive them because it is the only way back to peace and tranquillity. In effect, *I leave all punishment to God.*

I know that just saying "you must forgive your enemies" can be glib advice when you have been hurt very deeply. When does the hurting stop if your enemy just keeps on hurting you the more? Obviously, there are times when we must be assertive and call a halt to unnecessary emotional or physical pain. There are times when we must seek justice *before* we can forgive. But forgive we must, or else we will self-destruct!

How do I forgive? I've given a lot of thought over many years about what it means to forgive and have concluded that it is simply *surrendering my right to hurt back.*

Why must I do this? For one compelling reason: God has asked me to. In return, He offers me His forgiveness—the greatest gift anyone can receive. This is a more powerful stress reliever than any tranquilizer or blood pressure medicine I know of. I've tasted it for myself.

GOD'S PLAN IS FOR BUSINESS TO REMAIN UNFINISHED

This spiritual antidote for stress, I want to emphasize, is mainly for the benefit of those who are driven to accomplish some great task in their life. They are so compelled by a need to complete their goals that they are often cut short by stress disease. My message to them is simple: God is in the "unfinished business."

I once taught a stress management seminar to a group of ministers. They were in retreat high in the mountains, where God's creative beauty in nature was all around. I was there to show these ministers how to be better managers of their bodies and how to avoid distress in their very demanding callings.

Conducting the worship part of the retreat was a retired clergyman. He had seen many years of service as a minister and denominational leader, and though I had never met him, I could tell he was held in high regard.

We came to the last service of the retreat. To my surprise, this man announced that his closing message was to be a prayer. He then went on to say: "My prayer for you all is that *you will all die before you have finished your task.*"

At first, I was taken aback. "Die before you are finished?" What a horrible idea! What a defeatist attitude! I had been teaching these ministers how to *avoid* dying prematurely, and here was this retired minister telling them *to die before they're finished!*

But as that wise man began to unfold his understanding of God's plan, his point became perfectly clear. He was not praying for their early demise, but for a very long and fruitful life. His main point was that *God's plan is never finished, His work is never done.* He reminded us that in the great roll call of heroes of the faith given to us in Hebrews, chapter 11, *"all died in faith, not having received the promises"* (v. 13). Abel, Enoch, Noah, Abraham, Sarah, Isaac, Jacob, Joseph, Moses, Rahab—all lived "by faith," received wonderful promises of fulfillment, but "died in faith" *before* they had seen their promises completely fulfilled. They had to take God's promises by faith. "And these men of faith, though they trusted God and won his approval, none of them received all that God had promised them" (v. 13, LB).

Of course, there was a reason why these people died before they were finished. God is not a killjoy or a sadist who would rob us of final victory just for the fun of it! What was the reason then? Verse 40 makes it clear: "For God wanted them to wait and share the even better rewards that were prepared for us."

So what makes you think that you must achieve your goal and that you must finish all you want to do before you die? Do you have a neurotic need to prove something to yourself? Do you have some memory of rejection by a parent who said, "You'll never amount to anything?" Do you have some uncomfortable inner drive to prove you're perfect? Do you have a hope that people will respect you more if you are successful and powerful?

I suspect that the more we want to "finish before we die," the more likely we'll die before we're finished! Life is, unfortunately, composed of a chain of incompletes. We never quite finish the business of adjusting to one stage of it when we are pushed on to the next.

At first, this realization of the fragmentary nature of life can be very discomforting. No one really enjoys having his or her life chopped into a series of incomplete stages. Most of us dream of a time when all our pursuits will be crowned with closure, if not success. We hope for the time when the mortgage will be paid, our education will be completed, the redecorating will be finished, or the book written. If you are a Type-A person like myself, you are probably cursed with more than just a desire to see things finished; you are most likely driven by a *frenzied need* to see them finished.

Intolerance for delays and an obsession for closure will, unfortunately, make unfinished business hard to handle. *But you, too, will die before you're finished!* You're not likely to receive all that God has promised you in this life, either; otherwise, why else would you need faith?

Is it realistic to think that we can learn to accept incompleteness and still be content? I think so. *A successful life will always be unfinished,* and the more successful it is, the more will be left undone. This is how life works. It may seem unfair, but the positive side to all of this is that *God is with us in our incompleteness* and gives us permission to stop trying to accomplish everything in one brief period of existence. It is liberating to realize that *we don't have to finish,* all we have to be is *faithful.*

If you want to control your stress and reduce the pain and threat of distress, remind yourself each morning, midday, afternoon, and evening that you will *always have to leave something unfinished.* Place a note on your dressing mirror to remind you of this. Put a marker in your Bible pointing you to Hebrews 11. The "tyranny of the urgent" will be conquered if you give up on trying to run a race with an early death. You will then feel you have "permission" to put down that pen, pack away your paintbrushes, or leave that project until tomorrow!

Try "finishing" only that which *must* be finished now. Great buildings are built *one brick at a time.* Great poems are written *one word at a time.* Long distances are traveled *one mile at a time.* Try thinking of your immediate task as simply one step or one brick. If it is correctly placed and cemented then *that task* is completed even though the project is not.

Everything that is meaningful must be accomplished one little step at a time. Finish each step, take the steps one at a time, then relish the greater sense of completeness that follows. Then you'll live to be able to take the next, and the next.

Charles E. Hummel, in a booklet entitled *Tyranny of the Urgent,* points out that much of our suffering is due to our jumbled priorities. He reminds us of the great prayer of John, chapter 17 in which Jesus says, "I have finished the work which thou gavest me to do" (v. 4).

Hummel asks: "How could Jesus use the word "finished" when all He had was a three-year-long ministry? A few people got healed, some found forgiveness and a new life, but is that an adequate basis for saying "finished"? What about the hordes who still hobbled on paralyzed legs or rotten, leprous stumps? Have you ever tried to figure out what happened to all the broken people who were not healed when Jesus walked by? For every one who was touched, a hundred must have been at the back of the crowd without receiving even a glance of the passing Messiah.

And here is Jesus, coming to the last night of His earthly life. All around Him are hunger, disease, sin, and rampant misery. And Jesus says: "It is finished!"

The only sense we can make of this is to believe that when His earthly life was over, His *real work had only begun.* Jesus knew the Father's greater plan of healing and salvation, so He could resign Himself to the immediate, incomplete task. There was no feverish, frantic rush to do everything as quickly as possible because time was rapidly running out.

I venture to suggest that if you and I could also glimpse God's greater purposes, we would be less frenzied. We would be able to resign ourselves to dying before we're finished because, in a sense, we will have finished our immediate assigned task. We would not panic when we see our life rapidly passing away with so much left unfinished.

As I close this book, my prayer for you is also that of the preacher's: that you will die before you are finished with whatever grand and glorious goal you have set for yourself. I am grateful to this preacher who helped me gain freedom from the tyranny of time through this concept, which pointed me toward a more balanced life. I hope you will find, as I have, a deep sense of satisfaction—not so much in the completion of great tasks, but in the accomplishment of the smaller steps that lead to the great. Above all, I pray that whatever life you have left will be lived free of the destruction that stress works when it is left unchallenged.

Appendix

Keys to Figures 2, 4, and 5

Interpret your final scores for the stress tests on pages 34, 71, and 104 according to the following charts:

Figure 2

Total	Interpretation
0–5	You are definitely not a Type-A person. You may slip into Type-A behavior, but not often enough for it to be a problem.
6–10	You show occasional signs of Type-A behavior. You may have temporary irritation in your life, or perhaps some aspect of your work is getting to you. You are approaching the Type-A behavior pattern as you near the upper end of this score.
11–16	You show definite signs of being a Type-A person. At the higher end of this score, you are becoming prone to excessive adrenaline recruitment and are likely to be evidencing signs of distress.
17–24	Not only are you a Type-A person, you are living dangerously! Life may be miserable for you, or it may be very exciting. Either way, you are likely to develop cardiovas-

cular deterioration if you do not change your behavior pattern. If you smoke or have any of the other high-risk factors (diabetes, high blood pressure, or a family history of heart disease), I advise you to seek professional help as soon as possible.

Figure 4

Total	Interpretation

0–10 *No stress.* Are you sure you are alive?

11–20 *Mild stress.* You are basically healthy, but occasionally bothered by stressful life events.

21–30 *Moderate stress.* You should be concerned about your life pressures and how you handle them.

31–40 *Severe stress.* Your life is out of control and you probably need professional help.

41–60 *Dangerous stress levels.* You need immediate help.

Figure 5

Total	Interpretation

0 If you are sure you have been honest with yourself in answering the questions, you can rejoice. You have developed a remarkably calm and serene way of looking at life, and your reward will be better physical and emotional health.

1–4 You are probably in the safe range, but the lower the better.

5–6 Your stress levels are moderate, but you may still need to change some aspect of your life to avoid suffering some stress damage.

7–10 You are the victim of a lot of stress. If you don't make some changes soon, you may find yourself succumbing to stress disease.

Study Guide

Chapter 1: Understanding the Nature of Stress

1. What type of lifestyle lies at the core of the stress problem in our age?
2. How does stress cause illness?
3. What other problems are typically confused with stress?
4. Give examples of "hidden" stress in your life and discuss how you might better identify their underlying stressors.
5. Review again the reasons why even "good" things can cause "bad" stress.

Chapter 2: How Stress Does Its Damage

1. What is the major health problem of the twentieth century?
2. What are some of the *recognized risk factors*, besides excessive stress, that can bring on this problem?
3. Why are we often *unaware* of the sensations that can trigger stress hormones that ravage the body?
4. What *emotions* are particularly hazardous to our health because they trigger excessive stress hormones?
5. Discuss ways in which you can increase your *awareness* of the emotions listed in question 4.

Chapter 3: Stress as "Hurry Sickness"

1. Since most of us are a combination of Type-A and Type-B personality characteristics, make a list of those Type-A

traits and Type-B traits that *best describe you.* Share these with another person and see if he or she agrees with your assessment.

2. What changes could you make to your *lifestyle* to make you less stress-prone? Would this make you happier? What are some ways you can go about making these changes?

3. We often overlook the effect of *life change* on our stress levels. Make a list of life changes you have experienced this past year.

4. What is the most important *antidote* for "hurry sickness?"

5. How can you counteract the *tyranny of time* in your life?

Chapter 4: Stress and Anxiety

1. What are the two mechanisms that upset the balance of natural tranquilizers in the brain? Can you recognize these mechanisms at work in your own life?

2. Why are anxiety problems, especially panic anxiety attacks, likely to be more common in women today?

3. Review and make a list of the symptoms of panic attack, as they are described in the story of Peter in this chapter.

4. List six medical conditions that can cause significant anxiety problems that you, or any of your friends, have suffered.

5. What foods or drinks should be avoided by those who are prone to panic anxiety attacks?

Chapter 5: The Symptoms of Distress

1. What are the body's three major *protective* systems? Identify examples of each of these systems at work in your own life.

2. What happens when you *don't cooperate* with these protective systems?

3. Complete the questionnaire in Figure 4. Which three symptoms need to be given priority in your life?

4. What are the three *effects* of chronic stress?

5. While the temporary use of *medication* to reduce our stress symptoms can be quite helpful, why should we not depend solely on drugs to relieve the symptoms of our stress indefinitely?

Chapter 6: Are You an Adrenaline Addict?

1. To what types of behavior can we become *addicted?*
2. Why do we derive so much *pleasure* from these addictions?
3. What are the *dangers* associated with habit-forming behaviors?
4. How can we tell when we are addicted to our own adrenaline?
5. Adrenaline addiction can produce *withdrawal symptoms* similar to those experienced when you stop taking drugs. What are the signs of adrenaline withdrawal?

Chapter 7: Adrenaline and Cholesterol

1. Why are diet and exercise, important as they are, *not enough* to protect us from high levels of cholesterol?
2. What upsetting *emotions* can elevate cholesterol? How are these different, if at all, from stress producing emotions?
3. Why does intense or even moderate *competitiveness* produce stress, even though it gives us pleasure?
4. What *changes* could a person make to his or her life to bring cholesterol under control?

Chapter 8: Finding the Source of Your Stress

1. Name some of the more subtle or *hidden sources* of stress.
2. Why are these hidden stressors more likely to do stress damage to us than obvious ones?
3. For most of us, *people* are probably the most significant source of stress. Is this true for you? Who are these people?
4. As you use Figure 6 to analyze your sources of stress, pay careful attention to ways in which the *behavior of others* causes you stress. Why are they able to do this to you?

Chapter 9: How to Monitor Your Adrenaline Arousal

1. How does increased stress show up in changes to the *body's functioning?*
2. Why is it important to monitor how much adrenaline you are using to perform *normal* activities?

3. Of the four major changes that stress produces in the body, which is the *easiest* for you to recognize?
4. The temperature of your hand can reflect the degree of your stress arousal. Why does the hand get *colder* when we are under stress?
5. Prolonged muscle tension can produce severe headaches as well as other aches. How can you test your *muscle tension* to see if it is higher than it should be?

Chapter 10: Managing Your Adrenaline

1. How much adrenaline do we need in order to cope with *ordinary* life demands?
2. What are the conditions under which we legitimately need *lots* of adrenaline?
3. Make a list of the demands that typically confront you each day. Alongside each one write down whether or not it represents an *emergency*.
4. What are some of the ways in which we can lower our adrenaline when it is too high?
5. Quite often our "emergency" reactions are caused by *fear or anxiety*. How can you limit your fears or anxieties to a level that is not stress-producing?

Chapter 11: The Secret of Sleep

1. What is the most common cause of *sleeplessness?*
2. Why do we need more sleep than most of us realize?
3. Elevated adrenaline, such as that caused by an interesting activity, reduces our *apparent* need for sleep. What are some reasons for this?
4. What actually *happens* during sleep—both biologically and psychologically?
5. Review the *rules for better sleep*. Why should sleeping pills be reserved only for occasional and severe sleeplessness?

Chapter 12: Learning to Relax

1. Why is *relaxation* important as a healer and preventer of stress?

2. What three systems of the body can most easily be *relaxed*?
3. Relaxation should become a *lifestyle* if we are to control stress. What in our culture works against us getting enough time for relaxation?
4. Review your typical day and try to plan two or three opportunities for you to relax. If you are stuck at a desk, then plan on taking a short walk. Find ten or fifteen minutes, several times a day, to be alone for reflection and quietness.

Chapter 13: Changing Your Type-A Behavior

1. Can we change our basic personalities? What can we change about ourselves?
2. How can the *resources of your life* help you to make these changes?
3. Review the *four systems* for changing Type-A behavior tendencies, and identify which is the most difficult for you to change. Why is this so? (If you are Type B, think of a Type A you know well and answer this question with him or her in mind.)
4. Why is *laughter* an important habit to be cultivated?

Chapter 14: Creativity and Stress

1. Is creativity something we can *all* cultivate, or is it reserved for a talented few?
2. What are the common *blocks* to creativity, and how are these related to one's level of stress?
3. Each general level of adrenaline arousal has its purpose. What is *low arousal* best suited for? *Medium* arousal? High arousal?
4. Reaping creative thought is the last step of a series of activities. Review the other steps and discuss ways of implementing these steps you have found helpful.

Chapter 15: Spiritual Antidotes for Stress

1. A life entrusted to God can prevent a lot of unnecessary suffering. Does this mean that a Christian is *free of stress?*
2. The life of Jesus is a model of calmness and peace. Review incidents from the life of Jesus that illustrate this and reflect on how you might *emulate this calmness.*

3. Why is being "faithful" more important than being "successful"?
4. What *pitfalls* await us if we are too preoccupied with success?
5. What *spiritual resources* for coping with the problems of life do you find most helpful at this stage of your life?

Notes

Chapter 1
1. Schorr, Juliet B., *The Overworked American*, (New York: Basic Books, A division of HarperCollins Publishers), pp. 159-160.

Chapter 2
1. Cohn, Dr. Jay, *Science Digest*, April 1985, p. 31.
2. Meyer Friedman and Ray Rosenman, *Type-A Behavior and Your Heart* (New York: Knopf, 1974) p. 178.

Chapter 5
1. Published in *Biofeedback and Self-Regulation*, vol. 7 no. 1, 1982.

Chapter 6
1. Quoted from a speech given at a conference on addiction at Denver, Colorado, 1983.

Chapter 7
1. Quoted in *Science Digest*, April 1985, p. 35.

Chapter 8
1. Quoted in *Time*, June 6, 1983, p. 48.
2. Van Doornen and K. Orlebeke, *Journal of Human Stress*, December 1982, pp. 25-26.
3. *Science Digest*, April 1985, p. 35.

Chapter 11
1. *USA Today*, January 5, 1993, p. 1.

LaVergne, TN USA
23 August 2010
194296LV00001B/53/A